Vehicle hill tracks in northern Scotland

Adam Watson

An independent factual report on numbers, distribution, impacts, ground reinstatement

Sponsored and published by the North East Mountain Trust, PO Box 40, Aberdeen, AB11 6QQ, Scotland, UK, www.nemt.org.uk, NEMT Logo 'Tak Tent' (Scots 'Take Notice')

Published imprint: Paragon Publishing, 4 North Street, Rothersthorpe, Northants NN7 3JB, UK

First published 2011

© 2011, Adam Watson

Clachnaben, Crathes, Banchory, Kincardineshire AB31 5JE, Scotland, UK

adamwatson@uwclub.net

All rights reserved. No part of this publication may be reproduced, stored in a retrieval system or transmitted in any form or by any means, electronic, mechanical, photocopying, recording or otherwise, without the prior written permission of the copyright owners.

ISBN 978-1-908341-07-5

Book design, layout and production management by Into Print www.intoprint.net +44 (0) 1604 832149

Printed and bound in the UK and USA by Lightning Source

Front photograph: 'A scar on the face of Balmoral'.

Contents

	Page
Foreword	4
Acknowledgements	4
Introduction	5

Chapter
1. Hill tracks on individual estates in north-east Scotland 6
2. Hill tracks on Glen Feshie Estate 14
3. The 1980 regulations and since 17
4. Hill tracks in north-east Scotland since the 1980 regulations 20
5. Controversial new hill tracks outside north-east Scotland 47
6. Other new tracks in 2001–10 and others reported since 1990 59
7. Problems facing planning officers 66
8. Control of location, construction and reinstatement 68
9. Some examples of good practice 72
Bibliography 76

Appendices
A. Report on all-terrain vehicle track above Loch Etive (M. Newbury) 77
B. Site inspection of Rinraoich track, Rothiemurchus, October 1998 84
C. Removal of tracks on Mar Lodge Estate 86
D. Old Military Road, Corgarff, 2002–09 91
E. Balmore and Slugain tracks, Invercauld 104
F. Site inspection of Fungle track south of Ballochan 134
G. Author's correspondence with Chief Planner James Mackinnon 136
H. Critique of SNH 2006 report *Constructed tracks in the Scottish uplands* ... 138
I. Cairngorms Group 1974, *Bulldozed private roads in the Cairngorms* 143

Postscript May 2011, roads for access to the Beauly–Denny power-line 149

Foreword

It is now 37 years since 1974, when the uncontrolled spread of vehicle hill tracks on private shooting estates in northern Scotland led to much criticism and publicity by mountaineers. Despite this, new tracks have continued to be made almost wholly without public controls over location, impact and ground reinstatement. In the 2000s, the North East Mountain Trust and the Scottish Wild Land Group became greatly concerned at a new proliferation of unregulated tracks. The NEMT pioneered new methods of recording tracks by their members, and both organisations called publicly for better controls. Also the NEMT formed a Tracks Group of keen and increasingly well-informed members. One of them, Richard Gard, has digitised my original field maps and the resulting electronic maps were published by NEMT in late 2010, with Adam Watson and NEMT as authors and copyright owners (Watson & North East Mountain Trust 2010).

In the last few years, the Mountaineering Council of Scotland and other organisations added their voice, and a recent petition started by MSPs Peter Peacock and Sarah Boyack went to the Scottish Parliament and led to a debate in summer 2010. Minister Stewart Stevenson replied that the government would review the matter soon after the summer recess, but did not do this. In 2011, a new minister stated that a review would be done after the May election and would go for consultation. Hence the matter was delayed for another year at least.

This is an opportune time for the present technical report to be published by the NEMT as a detailed baseline and review of information. It should help elected politicians and government ministers come to new regulations that are fair to all and that minimise impacts on the Scottish countryside for the benefit of all.

Acknowledgements

For information I thank Bob Aitken, Neil Bayfield, Jim Conroy, Mike Dales, David Duncan, Kenny Ferguson, Richard Gard, David Jenkins, Gus Jones, Dave Hewitt, David Jarman, John Mackay, Ian Murray, Mike Newbury, Jimmy Oswald, John Phillips, Paul Richardson, Roy Turnbull, Bill Wright and especially Kenny Freeman and Dave Windle. I am indebted to soil scientists Alexander D. Walker and Rodney E.F. Heslop for discussions on technical aspects and time on field trips (especially ADW on numerous trips), Stuart Carrie, Simon Fraser, John Mackay and Chief Planner James Mackinnon for comments on planning, and Peter Holden about track removal by the National Trust for Scotland on Mar Lodge Estate. This book contains photographs by Kenny Freeman of tracks on Invercauld and NEMT members surveying, by David Duncan of a new Dalnaspidal track, by Adam Watson senior of an Argocat track, by Derek Pyper of the author surveying, and by Alastair Pout of tracks at Water of Aven. I am grateful for their permission to reproduce pictures. I took all other photographs.

Introduction

Having noted new vehicle hill tracks in north-east Scotland since the mid 1950s, I was asked in 1974 by the Editor of the magazine *Mountain Life* to draw a map of tracks in the Cairngorms, which he published. Later in 1974 the Cairngorms Group, a conservation body started by mountaineers in the Aberdeen area, issued a brief report wishing control of hill tracks. This led to publicity in the public media.

In 1977 the Countryside Commission for Scotland asked me to map tracks in the Cairngorms region, and I completed this with the help of staff of the Nature Conservancy Council, mainly at Achantoul in Aviemore. The CCS published the map in their report (1978) *Vehicular tracks in upland Scotland*.

During 1981, Jeremy Raemakers, then head of the Department of Physical Planning in Grampian Regional Council and later a Professor of Planning in Edinburgh, became concerned at the lack of controls on tracks. He asked me to map tracks in that region, and I did the fieldwork in 1981–82. GRC staff in 1984 produced standardised maps based on my field maps, for use by his planning officers. Also in 1984 my scientific paper on the survey was published by the *Journal of Environmental Management*.

Since then I have continued to note new or upgraded tracks, and walkers have given me information about new tracks they have seen. The current book is based on this factual evidence. As well as a detailed account of locations and impacts of new tracks, it reviews the technical problems of construction and environmental impacts. This leads to descriptions of the best methods to minimise impacts and maximise success in reinstatement of soils and vegetation. Such matters need public attention, because the report on *Constructed tracks in the Scottish Uplands*, a 'good practice guide' published by Scottish Natural Heritage in 2006, is so inadequate.

Chapter 1. Hill tracks on individual estates in north-east Scotland

In 1981–82 I surveyed vehicular hill tracks in and adjacent to Grampian Region (Watson 1984), and Grampian Regional Council's Department of Physical Planning used the survey to produce 1:50000 maps of the tracks in 1984. The survey was not a sample but a total survey covering the whole area. I paid for travel, fieldwork, analysis and writing from my own pocket.

The present section rests on the original survey. I record tracks on each estate separately, each estate's area of hill land, and total areas of grouse moor and deer forest in 1981–82. Briefly I describe construction standards. A particularly detailed survey was done of Glen Feshie Estate in Highland Region adjacent to Grampian, and I present this in the next Chapter, with a map.

The total length of known new tracks in the study area since 1982 is 166 km including wheel tracks, and a few of the new tracks took the line of former wheel tracks. This is small compared with Watson's (1984) total of 1151 km of new tracks in Grampian Region alone. Hence the original survey is still a useful database. Nonetheless, the later observations did not involve a complete survey as in 1981–82, and because of this lesser effort the 166 km figure may well be too low.

Watson (1984) described survey methods. An extra one used in 1981–82 but not presented in Watson (1984) was to assess each estate's area of hill land (other than loch, river, town, field and wood) to the nearest km^2 on Ordnance Survey 1:50000 and 1:25000 maps. I counted km squares lying wholly inside the estate's boundary, plus those with more than half of the square inside. The latter roughly balanced those with less than half inside.

Track length on an estate must be judged against the estate's size. Estate X might have twice the track length of Estate Y, but if Y covers four times the area of X, it would have only half of X's density of tracks per unit area. I therefore divided the total length of tracks on each estate by the estate's area of hill land, to produce comparable track densities per 10 km^2 of hill land.

Watson (1984) described ownership type (A - mainly absent, R - mainly resident, or I - institution). Each estate's main sporting land use on hill land was classified as D for red deer, G for red grouse, DG for both, or - not dominated by any game sport. This involved which main sporting land use occurred on most of the estate's hill land, not which one comprised the estate's main economic value or other value.

Main data

The Appendix below (Table 5) shows for each estate the length of bulldozed hill tracks, area of hill land, ownership type, and main sporting land use. Persons who were mainly resident owned most of the largest estates. Institutions generally had small estates, often resulting from break-up of former larger estates into smaller sections owned by insurance companies, forestry companies, the Forestry Commission (FC in the list), and others.

Hill land in Grampian Region covered 2300 km^2, of which 37% was mainly grouse land and 63% mainly deer and grouse (Table 1). In Grampian Region, 275 km^2 used for deer and grouse in 1981–2001 were for deer only until 1963 (Mar Lodge Estate).

Table 2 shows which estates bulldozed most tracks, with Invercauld leading and Glen Avon second. However, track density per unit area was greatest on Glen Buchat and Glen Muick. On both, grouse were more important than deer, and separate tracks led to most lines of grouse-butts.

Table 3 shows which estates destroyed the biggest lengths of former footpaths while bulldozing vehicle tracks, with Balmoral first and Glen Feshie next.

Table 4 shows which estates caused (by bulldozing of vehicle tracks) the biggest reductions of land >2 miles or 3.2 km from the nearest road or vehicle track. The largest reduction by far was on land now called Cairngorm Estate, including the three public roads to the ski area and bulldozed vehicle tracks on the area leased by Cairngorm Chairlift Company. In the Cairngorms massif and nearby, the new tracks in 1960–82 greatly reduced the area that lay >2 miles from a road or vehicle track (Fig. 1).

The longest penetration in a straight line by a bulldozed track into previously trackless country was 10.1 km in Glen Avon. The longest inside a National Nature Reserve was in Glen Feshie, an estate which also had the records for the longest in any NNR in the survey area (8 km), the longest in a straight line in a NNR (6.8 km), and the longest total distance of tracks in a NNR by one estate (17.5 km).

Construction standards

Tracks varied greatly in standard. Some were big trenches bulldozed through peat, with no side drains. Such tracks became large open drains and eroded rapidly. Examples were at 642813 north-west of the Cairn o' Mount, at 780903 near the Slug Road (now a plantation), and by the electricity board at 788900 near the Slug. The best tracks had a firm foundation with well-constructed drains on and beside the track. They have eroded little and a car can be driven on some (e.g. Glen Buchat).

Amounts of spoil varied much. Heaps were higher and wider where standards for track and drain were low. This often happened when contractors worked quickly, sometimes because clients requested this to cut costs. Three contractors told three clients that tracks made without drains would not last, but were ignored. An early track from Allt-na-giubhsaich Lodge to the col on Conachcraig below Lochnagar was built to intermediate standard. A later extension into Glen Gelder involved bigger spoil heaps, and was, and still is, a larger and more obtrusive scar.

Changes since the 1981–82 survey

Since the survey there have been few new tracks, but most have raised conflict, such as at Glen Feshie and Glen Ey. Despite a few changes, ownership and sporting use have stayed broadly similar up to 2011. A fairly recent ownership survey concluded that the main estates in the former Aberdeenshire (then the biggest county in former Grampian Region) 'are still virtually as they were in 1970' (Wightman 1996). The only big widespread change in use has been a loss of moorland to subsidised tree planting and to a far lesser extent to subsidised conversion to agricultural grass (Gauld *et al.* 1991), trends already evident in the 1981–82 survey.

Table 1. Area (km2) of hill land in the 1981–82 survey, with minor updating

Region	Deer	Deer & grouse	Grouse	Not dominated by any game sport	Total
Highland (part)	249	85	392	23	749
Tayside (part)	0	1016	139	0	1155
Grampian (whole)	0	1445	859	0	2304
Total	249	2546	1390	23	4208

Table 2. Estates with the 10 biggest lengths of bulldozed hill tracks in 1981–82

Estate	Length (km)	Area of hill land (km^2)	Length/10 km^2 of hill land
Invercauld	60	365	1.6
Glen Avon	49	177	2.8
Glen Buchat	39	47	8.3
Glen Muick	33	44	7.5
Mar Lodge	33	275	1.2
Glen Feshie	32	170	1.9
Invermark	29	74	3.9
Glen Dye	25	94	2.7
Balmoral	24	74	3.2
Glen Tanar	24	132	1.8

Table 3. Estates with the 10 biggest lengths of paths destroyed by bulldozed hill tracks

Estate	Length (km) destroyed	Length/10 km^2 of hill land on estate
Balmoral	22	1.6
Glen Feshie	21	1.2
Glen Avon	15	0.8
Invermark	9	1.3
Glen Fiddich	7	0.7
Mar Lodge	7	0.3
Invercauld	7	0.2
Glen Tanar	6	0.8
Glen Buchat	5	1.0
Atholl	3	0.1

On Glen Dye including Kerloch, bulldozing for forest roads destroyed 7 km of paths

Table 4. Estates with the nine biggest reductions of hill land >2 miles (3.2 km) from the nearest road or vehicle track in 1981–82, due to track bulldozing

Estate	Reduction (km²)	Reduction/10 km² of hill land on estate
Glen Feshie	88	5
Mar Lodge	81	3
Glen Avon	70	4
Invercauld	41	1
Cairn Gorm	36	16
Balmoral	35	3
Hunthill	28	5
Invermark	23	3
Glen Muick	16	4

Appendix (Table 5). Length of bulldozed hill tracks (km), area of hill land (km²) in 1981–82, owner type, and main sporting use, for each estate occupying >1 km² of hill land.

Region	Estate	Length	Area#	Owner	Main sporting
Highland	Glen Feshie	32	170	A	D
	Tulchan	21	58	A	G
	Dorback	21	51	A	G
	Cairn Gorm	9*	23	I	N
	Duthil (Seafield)	9	56	A	G
	Revack	7	51	R	G
	Lochindorb	3	38	R	G
	Dunearn & Lethen	3	41	R	G
	Forest Lodge	3	75	A	DG
	Rothiemurchus	2	53	R	D
	Castle Grant	3	53	A	G
	Invereshie	0	21	I	D
	Glen Ferness	0	18	R	G
	Dulsie	0	11	R	G
	Killiehuntly	0	10	R	DG
	Clava	0	6	R	G
	Inshriach	0	5	I	D
	Pityoulish	0	5	A	G
	Coulmony	0	4	R	G

Tayside	Invermark	29	74	A	DG
	Hunthill	14	62	A	DG
	Atholl	11	340	R	DG
	Tulchan	9	50	A	DG
	Rhidorroch	9	41	A	DG
	Millden	7	70	A	G
	Gannochy	7	48	A	G
	Nathro	3	21	A	G
	Fealar	0	53	A	DG
	Dalmunzie	0	25	R	DG
	Bachnagairn^	0	20	A	DG
Grampian	Invercauld	51	324	A	DG
	Glen Avon	49	177	A	DG
	Glen Buchat	39	47	A	DG
	Glen Muick	33	44	A	DG
	Mar Lodge	33	275	A	DG
	Glen Dye	25	94	A	DG
	Balmoral	24	132	A	DG
	Glen Tanar	24	74	R	DG
	Glen Fiddich	19	98	A	DG
	Kerloch	16	22	A	G
	Birse	15	40	A	G
	Delnadamph	15	31	A	DG
	Tillypronie	13	35	A	G
	Dinnet	12	56	R	G
	Edinglassie (Don)	11	44	A	G
	Mar	10	95	A	DG
	Altyre	9	29	R	G
	Park	7	14	R	G
	Dunecht	7	21	A	G
	Candacraig	6	33	R	G
	Glen Rinnes	6	29	R	G
	Cabrach	5	43	A	DG
	Ballindalloch	5	24	R	G
	Finzean	5	18	R	G

	Kinnermony	5	10	R	G
	Knockespock	5	11	R	G
	Clova	3	10	A	G
	Carron	3	14	A	G
	Easter Elchies	2	14	A	G
	Kildrummy	2	8	R	G
	Invermarkie	2	10	I	G
	Auchindoun	1	9	I	G
	Delnabo	1	15	A	G
	Glen Saugh	1	8	I	G
	Beldorney	1	9	R	G
	Glasslaw	1	12	A	G
	Glen Kindie	0.5	18	R	G
	Abergeldie	0.3	37	R	DG
	Knockando	0.3	18	A	G
	Fasque	0.2	14	R	DG
	Dallas	0.1	50	R	G
	Allargue	0.1	10	R	G
	Dunphail	0	28	R	G
	Littlewood	0	18	R	G
	Rickarton	0	14	R	G
	Birnie	0	13	I	G
	Douneside	0	13	I	G
	Glen of Rothes	0	13	R	G
	Cluny	0	11	R	G
	Drummuir	0	11	R	G
	Edinglassie (Deveron)	0	11	A	G
	FC Bennachie	0	11	I	G
	Kellas	0	9	R	G
	Rothes	0	9	I	G
	Arndilly	0	8	A	G
	FC Clashindarroch	0	6	I	G
	FC Tornashean	0	6	I	G
	Whitehouse	0	6	R	G
	FC Fetteresso	0	5	I	G

	Rothes	0	5	I	G
	Tilquhillie	0	5	R	G
	Brux	0	4	R	G
	Craigmill	0	4	R	G
	Fettercairn	0	4	R	G
	Lesmurdie	0	4	R	G
	Logie	0	4	R	G
	Ballogie	0	3	R	G
	Breda	0	3	R	G
	Corse	0	3	R	G
	FC Balloch	0	3	I	G
	Pluscarden	0	3	R	G
	Mormond	1	3	R	G
	Knock Hill	0	3	R	G
	FC Teindland	0	2	I	G
	Tillymorgan	0	2	R	G
	Brown Muir	0	2	A	G
	Brindy	0	2	R	G
	Druminnoir	0	2	R	G
	Findrack	0	2	R	G
	FC Drumtochty	0	2	I	G
	FC Rosarie	0	2	I	G
	Miltonduff	0	2	A	G
	Scolty	0	2	R	G
	Ardhuncart	0	1	R	G
	Bithnie	0	1	R	G
	Castle Forbes	0	1	R	G
	Corsindae	0	1	R	G
	FC Cushnie	0	1	I	G
	Balanreich	0	1	R	G
	Pittodrie	0	1	R	G

* Includes new public roads
\# 1 omit cases, mostly farms, where each separately-owned area is <1 km²
^ Included in Balmoral (Grampian)
Some estates have been largely converted to planted woodland since the 1981–82 survey (e.g. Dallas, Dunearn and Kerloch), and a few wholly or almost so (e.g. Bithnie, Knockespock and Park).

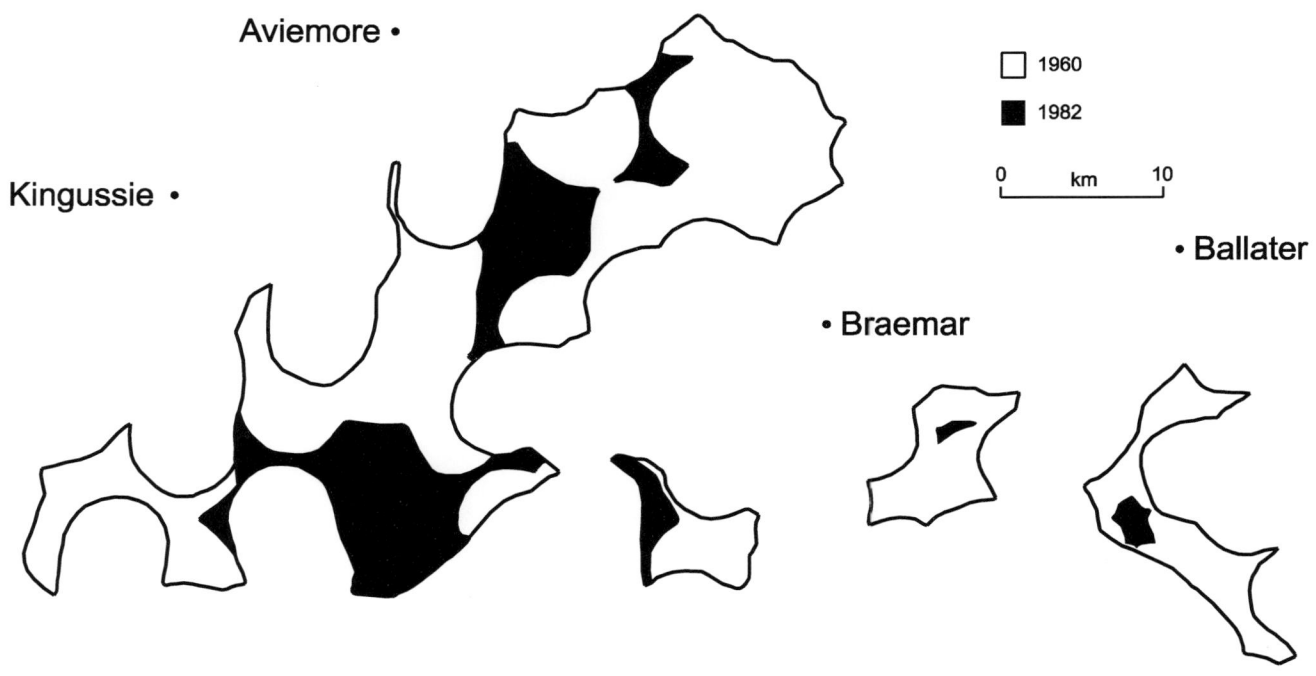

Fig. 1. Decrease in the area of hill land >2 miles (3.2 km) from the nearest road or vehicle track, 1960–82.

Chapter 2. Tracks on Glen Feshie Estate

In 1983 I surveyed this in detail. R.D. Watson, then Chairman of the North East Mountain Trust, was concerned about Lord Dulverton's proposals for tracks on the estate, and requested the survey as the factual basis for a report by NEMT. He later dropped his proposal, so NEMT did not produce a report. I regard it as useful to issue the survey now, updated. Concern about tracks rose again after succeeding owner John Dibben proposed roads for timber extraction, and new roads for timber extraction were mooted informally in 1996 by an agent of Will Woodlands Trust, which had bought the estate from Mr Dibben. Danish owner Klaus Helmersen of Danstruplund Holdings bought it in November 1997 from Will Woodlands, but he and agent Jorgen Smidt proposed no new tracks, as later confirmed for another Danish owner Flemming Skouboe who bought the estate in 2001.

I found the year of construction from aerial photographs at the Nature Conservancy Council's Aviemore office, my field observations, and discussion with local people. Fig. 2 is a map of the tracks.

Track A

This went from the glen bottom to the top of Coire Chaoil in grid square 8893, on the line of a stalkers' path. Photographs show that it was made between 1960 and 1962. Local information is that shooting tenant Peter Chevallier of Nedging Hall near Ipswich funded the work in 1960, two years before the Glen Feshie part of the Cairngorms National Nature Reserve (NNR) was declared. Photographs on 2 September 1964 show the track, before owners changed from Macpherson-Grant of Ballindalloch to Lord Dulverton (West Highland Estates). After track completion, vehicles travelled from the track end on to Carn Ban Mor, leaving wheel tracks in vegetation. The track lies entirely in the NNR.

Tracks B and C

Track B went from the top of Coire Chaoil north-east to Allt Sgairnich in square 9195, and C from the top of Coire Chaoil south-east to Diollaid Coire Eindart in square 9092. These two tracks across the Moine Mhor in the NNR were bulldozed between June 1967 and 7 September 1968, when George Chalmers was factor. Aerial photographs on 22 August 1966 show wheel tracks between the top of Coire Chaoil and Diollaid Coire Eindart, due to vehicles leaving prepared tracks.

Track D

This was bulldozed in the NNR from 847920 south of Ruigh-aiteachain to Allt na Leuma in square 8889, on what was formerly the most attractive part of the old right of way footpath. The track did not exist in June 1967, after Lord Dulverton bought the estate in late 1965–early 1966. The 2.5-km section from Allt Coire nam Bo upstream to a point just south of the bend at An Cagain (863898) was bulldozed between June 1967 and October 1968, probably in autumn 1968. Captain P. Kelley was factor.

By October 1971, Track D had been extended 3 km further up the glen, by bulldozing to 885891 close to Allt na Leuma. Mr George Chalmers was factor at the time. Severe land-slips and other erosion occurred at An Cagain, making the track impassable. This section was then bypassed by fording the river and making a short new track with minor bulldozing along the west bank up to a second ford, where vehicles could return to the original track upstream from An Cagain. Severe land-slips occurred after 1969 near the north end, south of Allt Coire nam Bo.

In attempts to solve the land-slip at the north end, more bulldozing was done up to 1980, including excavating into the hillside and the river. With more bulldozing, slope erosion increased. In 1980, stone-filled gabions were used to a form a river bank with a vehicle track behind them at a level place below the landslip, but a flood in autumn 1982 washed away the gabions and track. NCC then agreed to give funding to assist Lord Dulverton in further works on track construction in this part of the glen, but the estate later decided to extend Track H instead.

Tracks E, F and G

These were made outside the NNR. Track E was from the glen bottom at Carnachuin west to the Feith Mhor in square 8093, Track F past Lochan an t-Sluic west to Carn Dearg in square 8190, and Track G from above Lochan an t-Sluic south to Meall an Uillt Chreagaich in square 8287. All three had been built by 31 August 1964, before Lord Dulverton bought the estate. Wheel tracks comprised half (0.3 km) of Track F's first part, on freely drained ground.

Track H

This started near Ruigh-fionntag and ran south-east along the River Feshie's west side in square 8491. It was there on 31 August 1964, made by wheel tracks of vehicles following the same line on freely drained ground, outside the NNR. In December 1982, the North East Mountain Trust and Scottish Mountaineering Club wrote letters to the owner Lord Dulverton, as they were concerned to learn that he was considering major alterations to a bulldozed track. A flood in the River Feshie had washed away part of the track on the east side of the glen, and further landslips on the uphill side of the track added to the problems. A meeting was suggested, and a date and place agreed, but the estate eventually turned down the agreed date.

The estate in summer 1983 made a new track for 150 m up the west side of the River Feshie, bypassing the landslips on the east side of the river, and making a connection from Ruigh-fionntag eastwards to the original Track H. An excavator did the work by depositing gravel on the grass, the gravel having been extracted from elsewhere. The estate carried out these actions without seeking the planning approval which was by then obligatory above 300 m altitude in National Scenic Areas (the site was within the Cairngorm Mountains NSA and above 300 m).

When conservation and recreation bodies complained, Highland Regional Council asked Lord Dulverton to seek 'retrospective' permission. The estate did apply, and HRC approved retrospective permission. Lord Dulverton had claimed earlier that he had not known it was necessary to apply for permission. However, the letter from the North East Mountain Trust in December 1982 had given full details on the necessity for planning permission and the estate had replied to that letter.

The rest of the old track up the glen, 700 m long, was built up with gravel at the same time. Also, the estate constructed a new extension in square 8491 by gravel deposition for 550 m further up the glen, leading to a ford on the River Feshie. On the river's east side, wheel tracks continued beyond the ford for 200 m on freely drained ground to join Track D, after by-passing the landslip south of Allt Coire nam Bo.

Track I

This ran from the River Feshie at Carnachuin southwards past Ruigh-aiteachain in square 8492. It was there in summer 1964, having resulted from vehicles following a former footpath on freely drained ground inside the NNR. Another vehicle track from Carnachuin to Ruigh-aiteachan existed in 1946 and was not bulldozed.

Track J

This went from Ruigh-fionntag south up the west side of Allt Lorgaidh in square 8490. It was made before 11 June 1967, by vehicles following a former footpath.

Conclusion

The tracks, the largest intrusion into the Cairngorms NNR in its 57-year history, greatly reduced the wilderness quality of the west Cairngorms. The Nature Conservancy successfully opposed Mar Lodge Estate's plan to bulldoze tracks in the NNR in Glens Dee, Derry and Geusachan, but allowed Feshie tracks inside the NNR.

Table 6. Vehicle tracks on Glen Feshie Estate, B bulldozed, G gravel deposit, W wheel track), length to nearest 0.5 km, and in or out of the NNR. Omitted is a narrow 1989 track in the NNR for Argocat use, reportedly made by pick and shovel.

Track	Type	Length in km	In or out of NNR
A	B	4.5 inc. 0.4 wheel	in*
B	B	4	in
C	B	3.5	in
D	B	5.5	in
E	B	6	out
F	B	5.5 inc. 0.3 wheel	out
G	B	3.5	out
H	G	2 inc. 0.7 wheel	out
I	W	3	in
J	W	1	out

*This track was excavated before the NNR was designated, but was in the NNR after 1960, and is included in totals below.

Total length of bulldozed tracks 32 km, wheel tracks 4.5 km, gravel deposition 1.5 km, inside NNR 20.5 km, bulldozed in NNR 17 km, bulldozed in native pinewood 2.5 km, bulldozed on moorland 21.5 km, bulldozed on alpine land above 850 m altitude 8 km, furthest NNR penetration 7 km from Carnachuin as the crow flies.

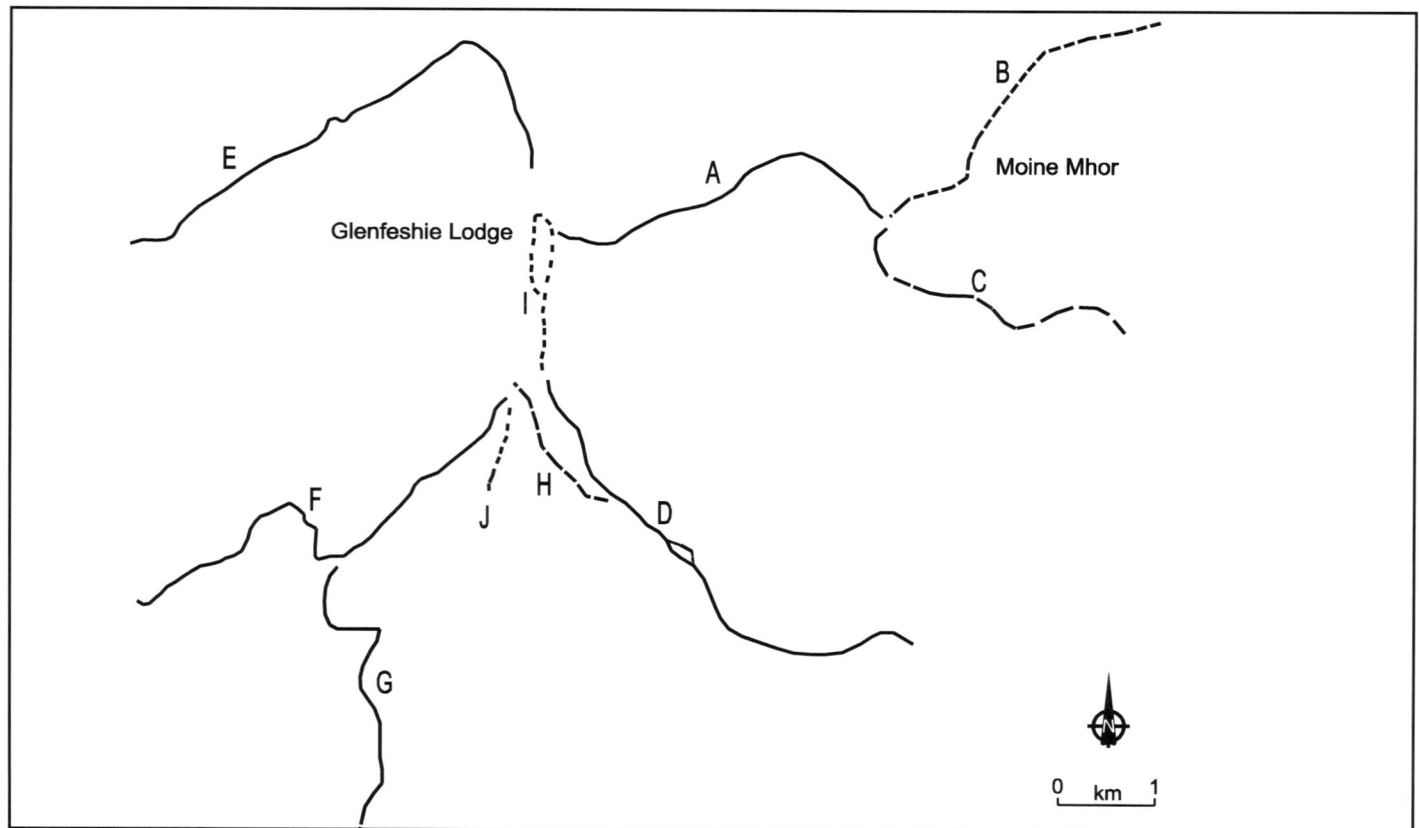

Fig. 2. Vehicle hill tracks on Glen Feshie Estate, surveyed in 1983. Small gaps between one track and another are inserted for the sake of distinguishing each track clearly on the map.

Chapter 3. The 1980 regulations and since

A useful summary of the Scottish planning system up to March 1996, with more detail on policies, official references, and year is in Tyldesley (Bibliography).

'Development' in the Scottish planning system was defined (The Town and Country Planning Act (Scotland) Act 1972, Sections 19 and 275) as 'The carrying out of building operations, engineering operations, mining operations or other operations in, on, over or under land....OR, The making of any material change in the use of any buildings or other land', the term 'material' being regarded as material to the objects of planning.

Planning permission became necessary for constructing new hill tracks for vehicle access above 300 m altitude in National Scenic Areas after the Scottish Development Department issued Circular 20 in 1980 (*Development Control in National Scenic Areas*). However, this did not prevent subsequent unauthorised new tracks there.

A defect in the 1980 regulations was that much of Scotland's finest scenery lay below 300 m and was still vulnerable to such tracks. In much of the west Highlands and islands, hills extend to sea level. The 300-m threshold was criticised for excluding tracks below that altitude in NSAs. A simpler alternative would have been to require planning approval for all tracks in NSAs. This eventually occurred in later regulations (The *Town and Country Planning (Restriction of Permitted Development) (National Scenic Areas) (Scotland) Direction 1987*), issued as Planning Circular 9/1987. Within NSAs, this removed the previous Permitted Development Rights whereby tracks for agriculture or forestry did not require planning permission. However, an exception remained. Tracks as part of woodland grant applications approved by the Forestry Commission were still exempt in NSAs, and still are.

The Town and Country Planning (General Permitted Development) (Scotland) Order 1992 (Article 4) allowed for the withdrawal of permitted development rights by a planning authority or the Secretary of State, with most Article 4 Directions having to be approved by the Secretary of State. Withdrawal followed by refusal or restriction of the development incurs a penalty of compensation to be paid by the planning authority, and this in practice resulted in planning authorities seeking a Direction only very rarely for exceptional cases. An Article 4 Direction merely requires that the developer submit a planning application, which the authority may grant, albeit with the possibility of conditions attached. Such conditions, however, may result in compensation.

Since 1996, the Scottish Executive has issued national guidance to local authorities and other agencies, on the topic of planning policy for new roads and tracks. National Planning Policy Guideline NPPG 17 covers Transport and Planning (1999) on issues regarding general transport, and Planning Advice Note PAN 57 covers Transport and Planning (1999) with Sections 41 and 42 on Building with the Landscape, Annex 1's Section 6 on Landscape Considerations, Annex 1's Section 7 on Natural Heritage, and its Section 8 on Built Heritage. Section 41 recommends that SNH's assessments of landscape are a useful guide for new development and particularly for choice of location. Section 42 states that new roads should, if possible, not cut across gradients and landforms, and that planning permission should allow for landscape character to be preserved.

Section 6 of Annex 1 is highly relevant, stating 'Consideration should also be given in rural and remote areas to setting limits to access by motorised transport, e.g. all-terrain vehicles, and to the associated construction of hill tracks.' Also highly relevant is Section 7, where it is stated that any development of new roads or tracks should have a minimal impact on the natural heritage, and that any maintenance, construction or restoration should be carried out to the highest environmental standards. The last phrase has been almost wholly ignored in the construction of new vehicle tracks and upgrading of existing tracks in north-east Scotland since the national guidance in 1999.

Dave Morris at collapsed track in Glen Feshie, June 1985.

Roy Dennis, Dave Gowans, Derek Ratcliffe at collapsed track, Glen Feshie, June 1985.

Chapter 4. Hill tracks in north-east Scotland since the 1980 regulations

Here I give information on new tracks in a survey area (Watson 1984) covering the former Grampian Region and adjacent parts of Highland and Tayside Regions. A cautionary note is that I have not done a total re-survey and indeed most of the hill land has not been checked. Nonetheless, new tracks made with excavators are so conspicuous that it seems unlikely that many were overlooked in areas popular with the many interested and concerned hill-walkers in the North East Mountain Trust.

However, it is possible for an estate to construct a large amount in a short time, as at Millden in Angus since 2005. Also, many estates in my 1981–82 survey are on low moorland hills that walkers seldom visit, and so new tracks there are more likely to be overlooked by walkers. Ordnance Survey 1:25000 maps published in 2010 show many tracks on such ground, tracks that were not there during 1981–82. Because of this and because my observer effort in the 1981–82 survey far exceeded that since then, the totals given below are minimal, and should be read as prefaced by 'at least'. Upgrading is even harder to detect, so some new cases of it may have overlooked. I would be glad to hear from readers who see new tracks or upgraded tracks not mentioned below. A cautionary note is that it can be difficult in a minor proportion of cases to decide definitely whether a track is a new excavated track or a new wheel track. This is because new wheel tracks frequently deteriorate in certain wet sections owing to vehicles cutting into the ground when soils are wet. This often leads to the estate taking action to upgrade such sections with an excavator, even though most of the track on freely drained soil remains in good condition.

New tracks known to me, including new wheeled tracks, total 166 km in length. On the main estates visited by many walkers, few new tracks occurred in the late 1980s and early 1900s. A large proportion of the total since 1994 involved Millden Estate in 2005–10, with 37 km of new tracks and 44 km upgraded by surfacing with gravel or by making new wheel tracks. The biggest total of new tracks on any one estate was on Invercauld, made over a longer period back to 1994. This followed a change in estate ownership from Captain Alwyne Farquaharson to a trust with a new factor.

1. Rothiemurchus, Gleann Einich, 1981

In summer 1981 the estate asked the Royal Engineers to repair 50 m of old track at the site of an early 1950s landslip that narrowed the track at Caigeann Beanaidh, a defile at 930055 and above 300 m altitude in the Cairngorm Mountains NSA. The RE unwisely used a big excavator on the up-slope and deposited gravel to widen the track, inserting wooden piles into the down-slope. The work caused more bare ground and left the area less stable. By late 1982, further slippage rendered the track impassable to vehicles and unsafe for walkers, and much gravel fell into the stream. The landslip has been unstable since. The estate did not consult NCC, despite the works being in the Cairngorms NNR, and informed NCC's officer at Aviemore only after work started.

2. Rothiemurchus, to the Cairngorm Club footbridge, 1984

In spring 1984, the estate excavated for 1.1 km a cart track west of the Cairngorm Club footbridge over Allt Druidh in the Cairngorms NNR and Cairngorm Mountains NSA. Despite this, no prior consultation with NCC took place. The track ran from 929077 near the footbridge to join the Coylumbridge–Gleann Einich road at Lochan Deo south-east of Achnagoichan. This widened the track considerably. It scarred ground by excavating borrow pits to provide gravel, by digging drains, and by leaving roadsides and surface as flattened gravel. This caused damage to prime Caledonian open woodland habitat, and some loss of such habitat. Although small-scale, this loss was on land seen by many visitors. Some parts of the track lay above 300 m.

During the work, 156 small pines and 128 medium-sized ones were killed, including many uprooted, and 16 more damaged. Drains were excavated for 80 m of track length, with side offshoots for 11, 11 and 12 m. At two places a metal pipe was inserted as a drain culvert, and covered with hardcore, but the ends were left exposed. The metal has rusted and is an obtrusion in an area of outstanding quality for landscape and wildlife. The pipe ends could easily have been largely concealed.

Flood moved a gabion (wire basket filled with rocks) from collapsed Feshie track, June 1985.

The work involved no saving or later reinstating of vegetation, topsoil and upper subsoil horizons. The operator left many turves upside down and buried others with subsoil. He dumped excavated boulders and peat on vegetation, which later killed it, and left many boulders upside down with the lichen-covered side underneath.

3. Rothiemurchus, Allt Dhru, 1984

This proceeded from south-east of the Cairngorm Club footbridge along the east side of Allt Druidh, following the line of the old Lairig Ghru right of way, to 937074. All of it lay above 300 m in the NNR and NSA. The track was widened, causing scarring of the track sides. In some places severe poaching of ground following blocking of former drains by the excavator driver. The length of track affected was about 0.8 km. The track remained in poor condition for years at places where water issues from the hillside. At 935073, where the track comes close to Allt Druidh, a flood which occurred after completion of the upgrading work washed away the track. This was associated with the loosening of the stream-side bank by the excavator. Vehicles coming down the track from the nearby 'cross-roads' of tracks and paths that is nicknamed Piccadilly therefore have to ford Allt Druidh at the washout site. They then must go down the west bank to another ford, and so back to the track.

Cases 2, 3, and 4 may not have been breached the NSA regulations, as they involved bulldozing to up-grade existing tracks, not to make new ones. Nevertheless the effect in the end was the same. The old existing track disappeared, to be replaced by a track as conspicuous as if a completely new line had been taken. These cases showed an obvious loophole in the regulations.

4. Rothiemurchus, Moormore, 1994

The estate applied for planning permission to make a track for vehicles to remove felled timber, from 937108 on the existing old track to Moormore house, westwards for 0.8 km to 931111 south-east of Achnahatnich. This was above 300 m altitude, within the Cairngorm Mountains NSA and the North Rothiemurchus Pinewood SSSI. The application was to excavate vegetation and soil down to the underlying gravel subsoil. The gravel was to be the road surface for haulage vehicles for 900 m. No prescriptions were involved on drains, retention of vegetation and topsoil and peat, landscaping of spoil and of track surface, or reinstatement. Highland Regional Council approved the application, and the track was constructed. It extended to the Achnahatnich fields.

Retention of vegetation and topsoil and peat, and their careful reinstatement, were not made conditions of planning consent, and reinstatement procedures were ignored. However, construction of this track did not cause severe impacts, because the route happened to lie on freely drained gravelly soils with a high stone content. Hence, problems from water, poor drainage and peaty soils were minimal, and spoil heaps were small and had sides of low gradient, so colonisation of the heaps by plants has been fairly rapid. Nevertheless, a far better result could have been obtained with less impact and better reinstatement of the existing mainly heathy vegetation, if adequate conditions had been attached to the consent. It is surprising that SNH did not recommend such conditions.

5. Rothiemurchus, Rinraoich, 1998

In preparation for a promotional event by the Land Rover company in late September 1998, Rothiemurchus Estate used a large tracked machine in mid July 1998 to upgrade an old track south of the River Luineag at Rinraoich, opposite the road to Moormore from the Glen More road, at 937102. This lay in the North Rothiemurchus SSSI and Cairngorm Mountains NSA. In total, 719 Scots pines and one juniper bush were destroyed, by cutting with a power saw apart from several uprooted by excavation, and the excavator altered fords at the river and at two streams. In total, the length of new track was 0.3 km and of old track upgraded 1.2 km.

Near the River Luineag, on a section about 70 m in length along a flush with rushes, much peat and topsoil were excavated down to the mineral soil and dumped in piles at the track-side and in a 7 x 4 m mound on top of classic blaeberry-cowberry-*Hylocomium splendens* moss vegetation below old pines. Much ground vegetation was buried along the line of dumped piles of peat and subsoil, and vegetation excavated from the track was mostly destroyed by being buried. No attempt was made to excavate vegetation, topsoil, and upper horizons of subsoil carefully or store them separately, or reinstate them in reverse order. As the excavator dug out a channel along much of the route, without proper drains, this created a large open drain with much mud and water.

Eroded track with fines washed out and many stones on to vegetation, Glen Feshie, June 1985.

'A scar on the face of Balmoral' (title of article by Chris Brasher, The Observer, 6 April 1980), Conachcraig from Lochnagar, track from Glen Muick in earlier year right, wider track from Glen Gelder in summer 1976 left, Crathie and Abergeldie woods beyond with Morven above, October 1976.

At the second stream crossing at 935097, a tracked machine excavated freely drained fluvio-glacial sand and peaty gley near the burn, down into underlying glacial till with a large content of clay. This created quicksand conditions in the clay, and left a steep southern gradient where water erosion cut small erosion rills by 15 October.

A detailed report from a site inspection of the track and tree cutting on 15 October 1998 is given below (Appendix).

6. Rothiemurchus, west Luineag to Bennieside, 1998

In August 1998, Rothiemurchus Estate upgraded a track from the Glen More road east of Coylumbridge at 919107 for a distance of 200 m to the River Luineag, including deposition of river-washed pebbles. The track continued for 1 km through a pinewood to cross Am Beanaidh at 919098 near Bennieside. The entire track was within the North Rothiemurchus SSSI and Cairngorm Mountains NSA. On 19 September there were signs that an excavator had sat on the Luineag's south bank, upstream from the crossing place, while removing gravel from the Luineag bed. The 1-km route was not an old track, but merely forwarders (openings) cut for timber extraction. Along much of the route, the excavator dug a channel without drains, so that the track acted as a drain. Along the remainder, it removed many boulders and stumps with roots.

On the excavated sections, piles of subsoil were dumped at the side, with many felled stumps and roots. Boulders and roots were deposited on subsoil or vegetation. A few old dead trees were moved to fall on vegetation, and juniper bushes and small trees were damaged and others uprooted. Large amounts of vegetation were buried under dumped subsoil, and other turf left upside down. No attempt was made to save vegetation, topsoil, and upper subsoil horizons separately, and no reinstatement was done on excavated material. At one point, a muddy pool on the track was left

South part of Conachcraig track to Glen Muick woods, Mount Keen beyond, October 1976.

with a short outlet to the river. The track surface was a mixture of mud and water. At the crossing of Am Beanaidh, an excavator cut part of the west bank on the north side to afford easier entry and exit for Land Rovers.

7. Rothiemurchus, Ord Ban, 1998

At Ord Ban close to the Loch an Eilein car park and within the Cairngorm Mountains NSA, an excavator in early September removed the surface of an old green track for 200 m up the first steep bank, starting north-east of 896086 and heading north-west. The entire surface on this steep section was now (12 September) a channel without drains, with erosion already evident. Many boulders and piles of topsoil and subsoil were dumped at the side, and some had rolled downhill. Further up, the excavator had dug up a section at a corner at 895088, and here and there further uphill as far as 894090 had removed boulders and turf. Most of the excavated turves were buried, and many lying upside down. The vegetation underneath areas chosen for dumping was not saved. Comments (two paragraphs up) about the lack of measures to save vegetation, topsoil, and upper horizons of subsoil at the Luineag route apply to Ord Ban also. The track surface was completely excavated for 250 m, and a total of about 200 m more in numerous small sections was partly excavated or had boulders and other obstacles removed by excavator.

On 19 September, Rothiemurchus head ranger William McKenna was working with a spade on the 200-m lower section, replacing some turves by hand. Already, turves were in poor condition, the excavation having been about a fortnight earlier. One might query whether it is appropriate for a head ranger, officially classified as a manager, to labour in this manner with a spade. The question arises whether this is appropriate, given that the estate receives taxpayers' money for the ranger service.

8. Rothiemurchus Estate, Allt Dhru, 2002

In November 2002 a track from Allt Dhru croft at 934073 was upgraded to 'Piccadilly' and then north-east to

Collapsed track in Rothiemurchus Estate, after 1981 army works failed, August 1985.

949083 at the junction with the road to Rothiemurchus Hut, a total of 1.8 km. It lay in the North Rothiemurchus SSSI and Cairngorm Mountains NSA, and hence consent from SNH was obligatory. SNH did not consent to the work, but the owner, as in the Land Rover event (above) did not comply with regulations. Despite SNH concerns about the specification, the FC ignored this and grant-aided the work as part of a Woodland Grant Scheme. Yet it was not done for forestry purposes but to 'improve' access for recreation. Contractors deposited hundreds of tons of surfacing material from Alvie quarry on the old track. The works converted what had been a rough meandering cart track in character with the landscape, into a manicured 2.3-m wide smooth road surface. Uniform in appearance due to the surface material of unweathered pale granite subsoil, it is monotonous as a surface for walking or cycling.

9. Mar Estate, Glen Ey, Aberdeenshire, west road, 1984

Mar Estate bulldozed this in autumn 1984 without seeking planning approval, although the site lay within the Deeside and Lochnagar NSA and above 300 m. For most of the distance, the route followed a former narrow vehicle track built in the 19th century, from 087883 to 088863. In a few places it took a new line, particularly on the first steep hill at the north end, where the gradients were lessened. It involved 0.2 km of new bulldozed road and 2.3 km of major upgrading of the old track.

Minor works would have made it possible to grade the surface of the existing track and make it safer for Land Rovers. However, the new road was built to agricultural and forestry standards in order to carry a heavy lorry, and so was very wide, with large cut and fill. Effectively, therefore, a wide new road was built along the entire 2.5 km. As usual with roads built to agricultural and forestry standards, turves and topsoil were not removed and stockpiled carefully and separately for later reinstatement in reverse order. Instead, they were mostly buried underneath the subsoil excavated for the road surface and the banks. The result was that the pale infertile subsoil formed a conspicuous scar across the predominantly dark colour of the heathery hillside.

Same place as previous photo, looking down to river Am Beanaidh, August 1985.

When walkers complained to Kincardine & Deeside District Council, the Council requested owner Captain Ramsay to apply for retrospective planning permission. After he did, KDDC gave approval with conditions on reinstatement.

The owner's agents wrote that the 'road is for all Estate purposes, particularly sporting (we have started feeding deer in the winter), agricultural (some improvement to grazings intended and grants expected), and forestry in the future (fencing materials etc.)'. It was expected that a lorry would take lime and fertiliser to old fields so as to improve the pasture for farm stock, and the owner applied for money from the Department of Agriculture and Fisheries for Scotland to pay for road, lime and fertiliser. DAFS staff met estate representatives on 14 May 1985. According to then-journalist James Hunter (*The Scotsman*, November 1, 1984), 'it appears that the Countryside Commission's reservations about developments in the glen are not shared by another official agency, the Department of Agriculture, from whom Captain Ramsay confidently expects a grant to help pay for the road which has given so much offence'.

In fact the main animals grazing the Glen Ey pasture for decades had been red deer, but DAFS did not make publicly known whether it paid the grant. On nearby Mar Lodge Estate, the Department of Agriculture funded a 4.5-km track in Glen Derry, years before the 1980 NSA regulations, supposedly for pasture improvement for cattle. Under Swiss owner Gerald Panchaud, the estate in the late 1960s claimed that the track was for agriculture, involving cattle in the upper part of the glen, and applied for grant-aid to the Department of Agriculture. I was told that the Department paid 60% of the cost. The estate put some cattle in upper Glen Derry in the first summer only, for a brief period of some days, and thereafter used the track for non-agricultural purposes involving shooting and deer management. When I attended a meeting to discuss bulldozed tracks, held at the CCS base at Battleby in the mid 1970s, a senior officer from the Department of Agriculture admitted privately to me that the grant-aid for the Derry track was abused, and should not have been allowed.

As usual with grants by DAFS, the Nature Conservancy Council and Forestry Commission, details were not published. By contrast, the Countryside Commission for Scotland published the names of all grant recipients, with details of what each grant was for and how much was paid. At first the new SNH continued the NCC policy of not publishing grant details, but then (1997) published them.

After KDDC paid a site visit to the Glen Ey road in July 1988, the Council decided that the results of the reinstatement work had been unsatisfactory and did not meet the conditions which they had attached to the planning approval. The Council agreed to request the owner to commission an independent study with recommendations on reinstatement works. By now the ownership had passed to a relative, Mr Mark Nicolson, who decided to commission the study (Watson & Bayfield 1988). He later implemented some recommendations in 1989, at a cost far greater than that incurred by Captain Ramsay in making the track in the first place.

The recommendations concerned hydro-seeding of the exposed banks, along with some minor hand works by spade to remove overhanging turves and place them in new sites on the lower parts of the cut banks. However, two difficulties for adequate reinstatement were the height and steep angle of the cut banks, and the infertile subsoil on the surface of the cut and fill. The result of the hydro-seeding was therefore not good, though better than if this condition had not been implemented.

10. Mar Estate, Glen Ey, east road, 1984

On the opposite side from the west road that raised the main controversy, Captain Ramsay of Mar Estate bulldozed a large, very wide road in the same season. This was constructed also to forestry and agricultural standards, and likewise formed a conspicuous scar of pale subsoil against the dark heathery hillside. It began near The Knock house at the foot of the glen beside Inverey, went up the east hillside to 094887, and then turned north to enter a woodland area at 094885. Its landscape impact exceeded that of the west road. However, although it lay within the Deeside and Lochnagar NSA, the regulations for planning permission did not apply, as it was part of an approved woodland grant application, and so counted as 'permitted development'. Nearly all of it went up a heathery hillside devoid of trees. Although it did eventually pass into a wood, a different line could have been taken in the wood, so reducing the landscape impact. A new offshoot led to a former peat track running far out on to the open hill, thus allowing vehicles easier access for deer shooting. The Forestry Commission paid for the road. The route involved 1.6 km of major widening and other upgrading of the existing track, and 0.9 km of new bulldozed road.

11. Glen Feshie, Inverness-shire, 1989

Owner John Dibben had bought the estate from Lord Dulverton of West Highland Estates in 1989. This case involved the excavation, said to be by pick and shovel, of a track wide enough for an Argocat but not enough for a Land Rover. The estate did not seek planning approval, but applied for retrospective permission after Highland Regional Council requested this. HRC then refused planning approval, and decided to consider an enforcement order to reinstate the area, in association with the Countryside Commission for Scotland, which had objected to the track. The Nature Conservancy Council did not object, because the track was said to be necessary for deer culling and NCC wished culling to continue. After the CCS merged with the much larger NCC into a new Scottish Natural Heritage, SNH did not maintain the CCS objection. The new track allows all-terrain vehicles to by-pass a gorge, and they can then roam far up the glen and hillsides. The new track's length was about 0.25 km, from the end of the former bulldozed track at 884891 to the crossing of Allt na Leuma to the east. It traversed a steep slope above the stream gorge so as to allow Argocats a safe passage across this slope and on to easier terrain on the open hill beyond.

12. Balmoral Estate, Aberdeenshire, 1992

The estate caused considerable ground damage in the old Ballochbuie native pinewood, using an excavator to widen and re-surface a former bulldozed track, and dig new culverts and drains. This track lay within the Deeside and Lochnagar NSA, and was above 300 m altitude. The length of major upgrading amounted to 1.9 km. No planning approval was sought. Upgrading was on the section starting south-west of 198896 and heading south-east uphill past the Falls of Garbh Allt. The work was done without saving excavated turves, topsoil, and upper horizons of subsoil. Many turves were left upside down and others buried under infertile subsoil. Several old pines had bark torn and branches broken. This would have been regarded as a 'damaging operation' had the area still been a Site of Special Scientific Interest.

Eroded track in pinewood, all vegetation destroyed, Rothiemurchus Estate, June 1983.

Formerly there were two SSSIs at Balmoral (the 1700-ha Ballochbuie and the 4290-ha Lochnagar, both described fully in NCC's *Nature Conservation Review* in 1977 by Dr Derek A. Ratcliffe). Dr Ratcliffe (personal communication) informed me that, after the Wildlife & Countryside Act was passed in 1981, all SSSIs in Britain had to be re-designated, and NCC staff began work on this for the two at Balmoral. However, the Queen's agents then informed NCC that the Queen was exempt, being above the law, and so the new regulations did not apply to land belonging to her. NCC did not challenge this, and so did not re-designate either of the SSSIs. SNH maintained this position. When SNH proposed EU conservation sites (Special Protection Areas and Special Areas for Conservation) in Deeside for consultation in 1995, they did not mention Lochnagar or Ballochbuie. The writer noticed this, and informed Rob Edwards, whose article on the subject in *New Scientist* led to much publicity in the daily press. This forced SNH to take a different stance. Although SNH had not re-designated either area by January 1998, they eventually did so and proposed both areas for EU designated sites. The areas should therefore receive better protection from damaging operations now than Ballochbuie did in 1992.

13. Invercauld Estate, to woods above Alltdourie, Aberdeenshire, 1994

Under its new trust management and new factor Simon Blackett, Invercauld Estate bulldozed a new 0.8-km track in summer 1994 inside the Deeside and Lochnagar NSA and above 300 m, on land that was formerly wooded and had been clear-felled. It began just east of Alltdourie farm buildings and headed NNW uphill to a point south of 165938, at the southern edge of a wood of old planted pine. In addition, the existing 2.3-km vehicle track from Keiloch to Alltdourie was widened and upgraded to take a timber lorry. The estate applied for planning approval for the new track. Neither SNH nor KDDC objected, and conditions with the approval were insufficient. The result was unnecessarily big environmental impact and inadequate reinstatement.

I inspected the site with R.D. Watson and roads engineer Douglas Stewart, in summer 1994 immediately after

Unusable track without drains in blanket bog near Cairn o' Mount, Glendye Estate, December 1975.

construction. The extent of cut and fill was unnecessarily excessive on the re-graded section to Alltdourie, and gradients of both uphill cut and downhill fill banks were too steep for soil stability and vegetation restoration. No attempt was made to save vegetation, upper subsoil horizons or topsoil.

One planning condition was that turves should be put on the downhill fill bank on part of the new track on a treeless slope above Alltdourie, to reduce landscape impacts as seen from the main road. Insufficient detail was put in the conditions. As a result, only a small minority of turves was saved, and the layer of topsoil excavated with the turves was far too thin, resulting in many roots being cut and poor reinstatement.

Some of the glacial subsoil used for the road above Alltdourie had too high a clay content. During the site visit, Mr Stewart and I agreed that this would be likely to cause problems later. This proved to be the case. After autumn rains, the surface became such a quagmire in places that a timber lorry could not use it, as shown on the TV film *Cutting Edge*.

Clearly, staff from SNH and KDDC on site visits had insufficient technical expertise on the inter-relationships of climate, soils, hydrology, vegetation and reinstatement, or on road and drain construction. I stated this at a seminar on hill tracks, held later at KDDC's head office in Stonehaven, and no one countered it.

At the time, there were reports that the estate may have received EU funds to aid this road construction. Shortly after the press published a letter by me drawing attention to the poor works, I received a postcard from Dr Allan Macartney, then MEP for north-east Scotland. He wrote that he hoped to see me and had information about Invercauld that would interest me. Our paths did not cross, however, and subsequently his many friends received the sad news of his sudden death.

14–22 and others. North-east Scotland, outside National Scenic Areas

Outside NSAs, some new tracks since my 1981–82 survey have caused scars in the landscape, as follows below.

Same track in September 1986.

14. Invercauld Estate, Westerton of Runavey, Perthshire, 1996

In summer 1996 the estate upgraded sections of an existing bulldozed track on heather moorland east of Westerton of Runavey in Glen Shee. The main section was on the fairly steep hillside at about 137691 on the Invereddrie part of the moor, extending to about 0.2 km. Other smaller sections were on the Westerton part near the mouth of the Green Glen of Allt an Daimh, and towards Gleann Carnach, amounting to about 0.2 km in total, mostly in square 1469. These works caused unnecessarily big impacts to vegetation and soils, and involved no reinstatement. The excavator had dumped boulders, smaller rocks, subsoil, topsoil and turves indiscriminately on live vegetation. It buried most of the excavated turves and topsoil, and the upper horizons of subsoil, underneath boulders, gravel, and infertile lower horizons of subsoil. Other wheel tracks of uncertain date since then have totalled 5.6 km, up from the Green Glen to the hilltop east of Coire an Eich, from Moine Glac an Lochain north-east to Allt a' Mhadaidh south-east of Sron na Fionnach, and up Carn Dearg beside a fence to Black Hill.

15. Invercauld Estate, Ben Gulabin, Perthshire, 1997

An existing vehicle track going up the east side of Carn Dubh below Ben Gulabin in Gleann Beag and on to the hill beyond Allt a' Charnaich at 105732 was widened and upgraded by bulldozing for about 2 km. The works caused unnecessarily large impacts. In particular these were the dumping of boulders and spoil heaps, the destruction of vegetation, the burial of vegetation, topsoil, and upper horizons of subsoil underneath boulders and infertile lower horizons of subsoil, and the failure to make any attempt to reinstate the ground. A large scar was made in this open landscape. The works caused considerable ground impacts at an unusual complex geomorphological feature on Carn Dubh, due to the route passing right across the feature, at 114721.

Track by Mar Lodge Estate on Beinn a' Bhuird, boulders rolled downhill, October 1967.

16. Invercauld Estate, Glen Baddoch, Aberdeenshire, 1997

In summer 1997 the estate upgraded 3.8 km of a bulldozed track up Glen Baddoch, constructing new drains and culverts, re-surfacing and re-grading, and making a larger turning area at the top end at 101790. These works caused unnecessarily great impacts to landscape, vegetation and soils, and involved no reinstatement measures.

As in the Westerton case (14. above), boulders, smaller rocks, subsoil, topsoil, and turves were dumped indiscriminately on live vegetation, and most of the excavated turves, topsoil and upper subsoil horizons were buried under boulders and infertile lower subsoil horizons. Heather and other plants that had colonised the centre of the track were destroyed. The track upgrading was associated with the estate's letting of the Baddoch shooting along with shooting by estate trustees and their guests including the Prince of Wales.

17. Invercauld Estate, Mammie near Gairnshiel, Aberdeenshire, 1997

In December 1997 a track of about 0.5 km length was constructed on to the 498-m hilltop of Mammie on Invercauld Estate, leaving the public road from Gairnshiel to Corgarff beside the start of the road to Clashinruich house, just east of 310 022. In this case the estate did not construct it, as it was made for vehicle access to a communications mast. Previously there had been wheel tracks made by land rovers taking shooters to butts on Mammie, and the ground on the route of the wheel tracks was freely drained with heather-dominated vegetation.

After removing heather turves and upper soil horizons, the excavator driver dumped these on top of living vegetation beside the track, where they will eventually kill most of that vegetation. A drainpipe was then inserted at a wet flush near the start of the new track, and then the entire excavated channel of the track was largely filled with stone rubble, though not up to the original ground surface. Hence, when I inspected the track in early January, it was already acting as an open drain and some washout of soil had already occurred on to vegetation.

Beinn a' Bhuird track too wide for vehicle, boulders not buried, vegetation destroyed, October 1967.

The rubble had been taken from a dump, as the material included many bits of thick wire and other pieces of metal projecting from the rubble, along with numerous broken red bricks, pieces of wood and torn plastic, and some other rubbish. In addition, the unnecessarily great impacts and total lack of reinstatement measures were inappropriate in a location so close to a lay-by and public road summit offering good views, where tourists often stop, on one of the main tourist routes in Deeside.

On an area close nearby and in view of the above lay-by and public road, all young pine saplings that had regenerated naturally were cut in December 1997 and left on top of heather. The trees were up to 2 m high and 10 years old, and so many were cut that they covered all of the heather over areas of several square metres at a time. This may have had no connection with the road-works, but added materially to the adverse landscape impacts caused by the poorly constructed works on the road.

18. Invercauld Estate, Gleann an t-Slugain, Aberdeenshire, autumn 1997, late 1998 or early 1999, and 2001–03

The existing bulldozed track up this glen ended at 135946, beyond which a narrow old cart track led to the ruined Slugain Lodge. Without seeking planning consent, the estate used an excavator in autumn 1997 to construct a materially wider track for 1.4 km up to 123950 in the glen floor in what is often called the Fairy Glen, along the line of the narrow cart track. This destroyed most vegetation on and beside the path, and unearthed many boulders, depositing them on the surface at the side of the track. No attempt was made to save vegetation, topsoil, or upper subsoil horizons on the area of the new track. On the western part where the track ran close to the stream, newly excavated subsoil and boulders were left in an unstable steep bank above the stream, and some pollution of the stream with silt and clay occurred. After enforcement officer Hamish Porter of Aberdeenshire Council's Planning & Environment Services wrote to the estate in December 2001 following notification by me to senior planning officer Stuart Carrie, the factor replied that the estate had carried out some 'running repairs' in 1997, an inaccurate misleading statement. Mr Porter wrote to me on 31 January 2002, 'The Planning Authority considers that maintenance of an existing track would not require planning permission, whereas the extension, alteration, re-routing or material widening of such a track would require planning permission for an engineering operation'.

Clearly the 1997 works with their material widening should have entailed a planning application, but the estate did not make one, and by January 2002 it was now too late for the Council to demand a retrospective application, because more than four years had elapsed since completion of the works (for the implications of this see Control of location, construction and reinstatement, below).

Later the estate made new vehicle tracks, as reported to the North East Mountain Trust by NEMT member Kenny Freeman in February 2002. The following account draws on a report by Cook (2003). Mr Freeman wrote that a track up the glen's east side has been extended 'in a manner which is very unsightly. Beyond the extended road, the former single footpath has become a double track to the head of Gleann an t-Slugain.' In total, 1.3 km of wheel track appeared on a former footpath starting at 130950 and continuing west along the edge of the ridge above Slugain Lodge to the fords north-west of the lodge, leaving heather and other vegetation on the middle line between the wheel tracks. This route showed some excavator works on its lower sections, particularly at bouldery places, and a few culverts on wet poorly drained spots.

The footpath is marked on OS maps, and was formed by climbers. Around 1997, estate staff began to use it with Argocats, running one side of the machine on the path and the other side on the heather alongside. This resulted in a double track, much wider than the original footpath, and later used by land rovers and other vehicles, after the above-noted occasional works. This included vehicles of the Upper Deeside Access Trust, used for carrying workers and materials to path-repair works further north towards the Sneck at the head of Glen Quoich.

In late 1998 or early 1999, a new vehicle track was constructed for 1.8 km up the northwards glen west of Meall Glasail Mor. Furthermore, minor engineering works continued for about 600 m to the north of the end of the excavated track, near to the watershed with the Gairn, and from there a 0.8-km spur of new wheel track to grouse-butts on Carn na Craoibhe Seileich. Also the estate made 1.3 km of wheel track starting at about 138945 in the main glen, heading for 1.3 km on to Meall Dorch, an east shoulder of Meall an t-Slugain. Both these wheel tracks showed evidence of excavator work in some wet or steep places, and in a letter of 16 February 2002 to SNH, Mr Freeman stated that the track to Carn na Craoibhe Seileich 'has been made up with hardcore for a substantial part of its length'.

Mr Freeman also alerted Aberdeenshire Council. In a letter of 12 November 2002 to Aberdeenshire Council, SNH stated, 'we are concerned at the construction of a new track and the extension of an existing track, both apparently without planning consent, and the possible impacts this may have had on the natural heritage'. On 10 February 2003, Mr Porter of the Council replied, 'In respect of the allegations made, Invercauld Estate should have prior to the work commencing submitted to the Planning Authority a prior notification of the development. No such notification was received'. He added that Council officials intended to visit the area, and 'If appropriate, Invercauld Estate will be required to submit a retrospective application for planning permission for this development'. In autumn 2003, the Council required this for the new track west of Meall Glasail Mor, but not for the others, and the estate submitted the retrospective application.

Having received the retrospective application and advice from SNH on reseeding and certain measures to reduce the landscape impact and aid reinstatement, the Planning Service eventually recommended acceptance, with conditions on the reinstatement. At the Marr Committee meeting of Aberdeenshire Council on 13 December 2005, Kenny Ferguson and Kenny Freeman of NEMT spoke to the Committee as objectors, and Simon Blackett the estate manager spoke in favour of the permission. One Councillor then called for rejection, was backed and seconded by another Councillor, and the Committee unanimously refused permission. This received considerable publicity in the press, and a fuller account summarising the issue of the Slugain track has been published (Cook 2006).

After a refusal by a Council, a developer has the right to appeal against this decision, and in this case the estate could do so up to September 2006. If the estate were not to appeal, the Council then is allowed the option of taking enforcement action. In fact, however, the list of Appeals Lodged with Scottish Ministers in the Week Ending 11

Invercauld Estate at Ballachrosk, Glen Gairn, steep line on left abandoned, October 1981.

Adam Watson senior in eroded drain, near-vertical cut, Ballachrosk, October 1981.

Adam Watson senior at collapsed Ballachrosk track, culvert too narrow, October 1981.

August 06 contains Appeal No APP/2003/0210, a written submission by Invercauld Estate, Agent Ryden LLP, 1 Albyn Terrace, Aberdeen, Appeal Against Refusal of Full Planning Permission for Engineering Works to Form Hill Track and Borrow Pit (Retrospective) at Hill Track Gleann An T-Slugian (sic), Braemar, Ballater NO 3147 7945.

Soil and water washed on to public road from Ballachrosk track, October 1981.

This appeal was expected by many, because the estate's tenant had earlier appealed successfully against enforcement by Aberdeenshire Council at Balmore-Auchtavan. This quashing of the enforcement notice and award of full planning consent with minor irrelevant conditions was due to an Inquiry Reporter's decision letter of 22 September 2005 that revealed a surprising lack of grasp of the technical issues. Examples are, 'Requiring removal of all imported material to source is excessive. The resulting damage would be greater than the works carried out', 'The works have had minimal landscape and visual impacts', 'Nor is there evidence to demonstrate that the works as carried out have created a feature that will in future be vulnerable to soil erosion', 'the works have not entailed a greater degree of engineering or earthworks than is reasonably necessary', 'it is not clear to me to what extent the works could have been modified to reduce their impact while retaining their purpose', and 'it has not been demonstrated that the purpose of the works could have been achieved in a manner that would have had a significantly reduced impact on their surroundings'.

All these and many other statements in the decision letter demonstrate profound ignorance of the subject. The public can therefore have no confidence that the appeal at Slugain will receive a proper critical technical appraisal by a Scottish Executive Inquiry Unit Reporter, particularly since in the Slugain case the Aberdeenshire Planning Service had unwisely recommended planning permission, with only minor conditions on reinstatement. In the event, the SEIRU Reporter in late 2006 quashed the AC refusal of permission, again with minor conditions on reinstatement.

19. Invercauld Estate, Meall Odhar, early 1999

Glenshee Chairlift Company already had a bulldozed vehicle track from the car park to the top of Meall Odhar, and estate vehicles used this to gain access to a spur which ran south from the top of the first steep slope up from the Meall Odhar café. Since the spur had freely drained soils, the vehicles ran along the top of the spur, making fairly inconspicuous wheel tracks along the same route. In 1999, however, the estate used a excavator to make conspicuous deep cross-drains on the existing track. Vegetation, topsoil and peat were dumped indiscriminately amongst excavated subsoil and stones, with no attempt at reinstatement. On the steeper sections, the new drains were dug so deeply that considerable scouring by water, and associated erosion of sediment on to vegetation downhill, had already occurred by July. An excavator driver in early summer 2002 caused further ground damage by digging deeper cross-drains and nearby longitudinal drains on the uphill slope. Along the spur, the bulldozer in 1999 shaved off vegetation for about 0.5 km along the track route (mostly lichen-rich heather) and the thin layer of topsoil, dumping both vegetation and topsoil at the side on top of other vegetation. There was no need for any work on the spur, and the track surface of subsoil is now far more conspicuous than the former narrow wheel tracks.

20. Invercauld Estate, Meall Odhar, Aberdeenshire, 2002

In the annual monitoring report (A. Watson 2002, Glenshee Ski Area, summer inspection - 1st August 2002), I stated (p. 1), 'The vehicle track up the first slope of Meall Odhar Mor above the Meall Odhar cafe has been re-routed by the estate in one place, involving bulldozing a new line in a short section to reduce the gradient, with spoil deposited at the side. This encroaches on the south side of the ski run. Two snow fences previously stood at the south side of the run, with a gap between them. The north limit of the new road's running surface penetrates for 0.3 m north of the line between the two fences. Northwards beyond this, a bank of spoil penetrates 3 m into the ski run, and then a number of excavated boulders which rolled 10–12 m downhill into the middle of the ski run, where they lie on the vegetation. In 2001 and 2002 the estate excavated deep cross-drains on the track up Meall Odhar Beag and the one up Meall Odhar Mor, removing existing wooden box-drains inserted earlier by the Company and leaving them on the vegetation at the side. One of the 2002 drains at a corner on the Meall Odhar Mor track was left with its lowest point in mid-air close to the burn. The exit point should have been cut less steeply, and should be built up now with interlocking boulders.'

21. Invercauld Estate, Creagan Bheithe and Ben Gulabin, Gleann Beag, Perthshire

This new track began near a hut north of the col between Ben Gulabin and Creagan Bheithe. It extended 1.6 km north to grouse-butts on Carn Mor. In November 2002, Bill Wright of the Cairngorms Campaign took a photograph of it, and reported no plant growth on the bared ground. It may have been made in 1997 along with track 15's upgrading. In 2008 a 2.6-km extension of new track passed a new hut at 106756 north-west of Carn Mor to 104757 and then turned south-west to 097750. Since then, a 2.3-km track has extended towards Carn a' Gheoidh and then downhill along the north side of Allt Coolah. In addition, a new track was excavated for 0.6 km in approximately a straight line, starting on the west side of the lower part of the burn between Ben Gulabin and Carn Dubh, south-west to 105723 and diverging further from the burn as it gained altitude. The excavation involved a ditch c. 1 m deep, subsoil deposited on top of vegetation to produce a track c. 1.5 m wide, and on the other side of the ditch a mixture of excavated peat and turves dumped on top of vegetation. The ditch is eroding, and because the track was raised above surrounding ground, it is highly obtrusive. From 105723 an extension turns south for 200 m with substantial excavation and then 300 m of wheel track to Ben Gulabin.

22. Invercauld Estate, Bealach Dearg, Aberdeenshire, 2001

This involved upgrading of a former track for 0.9 km from near a hut on the high saddle to the low part of Allt na Claise Moire. Andrew Hyams referred to it as 'This year's abomination' in a letter to *The Angry Corrie* (2001, 51, p. 19). Invercauld factor Simon Blackett responded (*The Angry Corrie* 2001, 52, p. 18) with a letter explaining that 'The recent maintenance work, following damage caused to the road by unusually heavy rain, may give the impression that this is a newly created road'.

23. Invercauld Estate, Balmore to Auchtavan, Aberdeenshire, spring 2005

The shooting tenant of this part of Invercauld Estate, Mr Pennel, requested a contractor to use an excavator to widen this existing track and to construct drains, without applying for planning consent. The affected section started at the far side of the bridge north-east of Balmore within the Deeside and Lochnagar NSA, and continued almost to Auchtavan, for about 2 km. In addition, from a junction at 215950, upgrading was done in an easterly direction for the first 200 m of an old track that heads uphill past the derelict Loin farm to grouse-butts. A small amount of upgrading by excavator, of about 100–200 m, was also done then or in very recent years in the area of the zigzags north of Loin, and likewise on a short section of track at Creag Bhalg north of Auchtavan.

Furthermore, a new section of track was made in 2005 from the far side of the bridge north-east of Balmore in an easterly direction uphill through the birch wood for 200 m to a field where red-legged partridges were reared for release for shooting. This also was within the Deeside and Lochnagar NSA.

Because the engineering works on the Balmore–Auchtavan track constituted a clear breach of planning regulations, the Marr Planning Inspector of Aberdeenshire Council, Mr Hamish Porter, served enforcement notices, to stop the works at the earliest possible date and thereby prevent further damage. Although Invercauld Estate owned the land, the shooting tenant Mr Pennel carried out the works to ease access for shooting. There was therefore no permitted development right under the General Permitted Development Order, which allows tracks for forestry and agriculture.

Mr Pennel (letter dated 21 June 2005) then appealed against the enforcement notices rather than apply for retrospective planning permission. A Public Inquiry (PI) followed, and the PI Reporter R.W. Maslin on 22 September 2005 sent his decision letter, which quashed the enforcement notices and gave planning permission for the works. The only conditions were that a scheme for reseeding should be submitted to Aberdeenshire Council, and then carried out and checked for its success.

Many of the Reporter's main comments revealed ignorance of the technical aspects of the subject. I therefore arranged a site visit in November 2005 by two retired soil scientists and myself. Our report on this visit is in the Appendix below.

Planning officers in the Cairngorms National Park Authority were concerned by the Reporter's quashing of the enforcement notices, and welcomed receiving a copy of our Balmore report (email from Andrew Tait). The CNPA had submitted representations, but the Reporter did not take account of these in his report, and hence they were ignored in the decision. The reporter failed to recognise the National Park and its aims as a material consideration when determining the appeal against enforcement, even though the Reporter was made aware of the fact that the site lay within the Park. Because of this, the CNPA decided to appeal against the Reporter's decision, and preliminary exchanges had taken place by mid December 2005. I was informed on 17 November 2005 by the Marr Planning Inspector that he understood that the CNPA were to pursue a Judicial Review on this matter, and in January the Chairman of the North East Mountain Trust, Jennifer Cook, learned in a letter from the Scottish Executive's Chief Planner that it was the subject of an appeal at the Court of Session.

On 10 November 2006, Andrew Tait informed me in writing that the Court of Session had upheld the CNPA's challenge and had quashed the Reporter's decision. The matter would therefore come again to the Reporters Unit for redetermination. On 13 November I sent a copy of the site investigation report of November 2005 to the Reporters Unit so that they could be fully appraised on the technical issues. Following the news about the decision of the Court of Session, the authors of that site report produced a critique of the Reporter's decision letter of September 2005, which is also in the Appendix below. Also I wrote to Mike Rumbles MSP, stating that a different Reporter must be allocated to the redetermination, so as to provide a reasonably independent impartial view.

A different Reporter was subsequently allocated, made a site visit, and then held a hearing at Ballater, attended by the appellants' agents and the objectors. The above three authors wrote a page of technical recommendations and sent this to the Reporters Unit before the hearing, but did not attend the hearing because they were neither objectors nor backers of the development. The decision letter of 8 May 2008 was on the whole in favour of the Council and against the applicant. The estate was ordered to follow almost all of the above recommendations, as well as a few indicated by the CNPA and SNH. This was a useful outcome, which should greatly reduce the impact of the works on the landscape, and should increase reinstatement materially. So far, however, little reinstatement work has been done.

24. Atholl Estate, Glen Bruar, Perthshire

A new 2-km track obliterated a footpath up Allt Sheicheachan from a bothy, and a 1.5-km extension on to Beinn a' Chait occurred 'recently' (Catherine Moorehead 2002, *The Angry Corrie*, No 54, p. 19).

25. Glen Isla Estate, Craig Lair, Angus, 2002

A track goes from Fergus north-east to a shooters' hut. Beyond, a footpath went up for 1 km, but has been obliterated by a bulldozed track. A track for 4 km on a new line was made up Craig Lair to Mid Hill and then south-west to join an old bulldozed track beside Alltgillie Burn.

26. Glen Isla Estate, Monamenach, Angus, 2002

A former bulldozed track ran from Auchavan west up the burn for 1.3 km to beside a col south-east of Monamenach. The track surface eroded greatly in recent years, and in 2002 a bulldozer excavated a new widened line along the same route.

27. Candacraig Estate, Old Military Road, Corgarff, Aberdeenshire, 2002

The estate (factor Robin Leslie Melville of Savills, Brechin) upgraded this ancient road, obliterating almost all of it on a 2-km section, without seeking planning consent. A more detailed report from site visits is given below.

28. Candacraig Estate, other tracks, Aberdeenshire, 2002

In summer 2002 the estate carried out upgrading for 2.5 km on former tracks to grouse-butts. The route began on the public road south of Boilhandy, went north of The Craig, and continued into the Conrie catchment south of Tom a' Bhuraich. Other former tracks for at least 3 km were upgraded out of Glen Conrie, on to Litte Scraulac and Cairnagour. The exposed gravel on one of the widened tracks forms a conspicuous scar as seen from the main road at Roughpark. All these works involved no application for planning consent.

29. Reidhaven Estate, east of Dava, Morayshire, mid 1980s

The estate bulldozed this 1.1-km track on Carn Biorach near Dava Bridge, along the line of a former track to Aittendow farm, which has been unoccupied in recent decades. Excavation left big spoil heaps on either side of the track. These heaps were of contrasting pale subsoil and dark peat, conspicuous at a distance.

30. Reidhaven Estate, above Foregin, Carr Bridge, 1992–93

An old track led through former fields from East Foregin to a ruined farm at the north end of the fields at 875257. In the mid 80s the estate upgraded this track for 0.8 km and extended a new 1.2-km track on the moorland above, to grouse-butts on the lower slope of Carn a' Chuaille and then north-west uphill to Allt na Criche. In 1992–93 the estate applied to extend and re-align the upper parts of this track, because of erosion resulting from poor initial construction (Aitken 1995). Aitken stated (p. 20) 'The aim was to resolve gross drainage problems on a long incut section of track running straight uphill at high gradient, which holds deep snow till late in the season, collects large volumes of surface water and groundwater, and forms a scar highly conspicuous from the A9. This track had been constructed with scant understanding or consideration of the conditions, and with no regard for its landscape impact. I suggested a realignment to reduce the grade and the visibility of the track and to help restore the redundant line, but the cost would have been considerable. Apparently as a result of a change in estate ownership, no work has been done'. The track formed a pale zigzag scar which in autumn 2002 was still highly prominent from the Cairngorms even 27 km to the south, as well as to those using the A9 Perth–Inverness road along the glen below the hillside with the track.

31. Mar Lodge Estate, Bynack, 1990

This case raised controversy, close to the Cairngorm Mountains NSA. By 1988 the estate had bulldozed a track south of Bynack Lodge on the line of the former right-of-way path to Glen Tilt, for 1.6 km to 999840. They then upgraded part of it, using an excavator to dig gravel from Allt an t-Seilich and deposit it on the track. A walker alerted KDDC. At the request of planning officer Roger Eames, James W.H. Conroy made a site visit and wrote a brief report (29 October 1990) for the North East Mountain Trust (*Report of visit to the area of Bynack/Geldie to examine constructed track - 13 October 1990*). He found three places where gravel had been removed from the burn, including one showing the imprint of the excavator bucket, as seen in a photograph. On 14 February 1991, Mr Eames sent a letter on 'Alleged roadworks at Bynack/Geldie' to estate factor Toby Metcalfe of Smiths Gore, Fochabers. In it he stated, 'I shall leave this for your consideration meantime and arrange for a site inspection in the spring following which I shall have to form an opinion as to whether development requiring express planning permission has occurred'. In the end, KDDC took no action. Clearly, estates could circumvent regulations by arguing that the works did not involve bulldozing a new track.

32. Forest Enterprise, Corrie of Fee, Glen Doll, Angus, spring 1999

This was within the Deeside and Lochnagar NSA. Mike Newbury (Appendix A) describes this new vehicle track excavated along the line of a former footpath, and Maison (1999) gives further detail. The original path went through a plantation owned by Forest Enterprise, and 'had become badly eroded due to the tramping of many feet' (Maison). In my view the heavy use was a necessary condition, but not sufficient. The wet churned path occurred largely due to the dense dark trees blocking off the drying effects of wind and sun, as in the nearby plantation north of Moulzie. Maison wrote 'Apparently a recent survey identified parts of the path within the corrie as requiring repair/upgrading. It is believed that following this survey SNH initiated the proposal to upgrade the existing path within the forest which leads into Corrie Fee. Forest Enterprise subsequently applied to SNH for a grant in order that they may comply with the request. Forest Enterprise stated that the path was to be upgraded to facilitate the extraction of deer and the mending of fences, whilst SNH give the impression that it was to assist the path contractors during their efforts with regards to the path within the corrie. This was all very strange when one considers that no machinery or vehicle intrusion is permitted within the SSSI.'

'Another anomaly is the fact that the materials required to repair the path are allegedly to be flown in from Bachnagairn, so why create this monstrosity in the first place? Maybe the truth will out sometime in the future. The path, which was built to a brief specification, can only be described as an eyesore and now requires urgent remedial works. It is 580 metres in length and was laid at a cost of £10 per metre.'

'It will probably cost in the region of £20 per metre to eliminate the damage and make the path usable to the walking public. Obvious faults are poorly constructed drains, which are probably impassable for vehicles and dangerous to hill goers. Insufficient detail to landscaping, stumps protruding from the ground which may be dangerous, and a general appearance that the whole contract was carried out at speed and without thought of the damage to the environment. I am pleased to report that Mike Dales and Mike Newbury of the Mountaineering Council of Scotland visited the locus of the works recently and have undertaken to pursue the matter on behalf of the hill-walking public.'

Subsequently, Newbury (*The Scottish Mountaineer* 2002, No 12, p. 37) stated that the MC of S had complained to landowner Forest Enterprise and 'demonstrated in detail the need for complete reconstruction of another ugly track at Corrie Fee (Glen Clova) and this has been completed'.

It is noteworthy that FE did not apply for planning approval in this case or the Loch Etive one, though they subsequently did apply for retrospective permission to Angus Council and Argyll & Bute Council after the MC of S complained.

33. New track on Culblean, Dinnet Estate, August 2003

A local resident reported this to Aberdeenshire Planning Service soon after bulldozing. The *Press & Journal* on 19 August 2003 carried a headline 'Hill track on grouse hill to be probed', quoting the resident saying the track was 'a huge golden triangle'. The reporter noted that the area was in an SSSI on Dinnet Estate, owned by Edward Humphrey. The journalist spoke to the owner's father and former owner Marcus Humphrey, Aberdeenshire Councillor for Upper Deeside, who in spring 2003 had tried to become a Council nominee on the Cairngorms National Park Board, but had been outvoted. The journalist wrote that the Planning Service would investigate the track. In sunlight it was visible to the naked eye at 20 km range near Banchory, and very conspicuous around Dinnet and Logie Coldstone. It lay in the Cairngorms National Park. Freshly exposed subsoil from dark pink granite caused the bright orange colour. A track was there before, but the operator widened and re-graded it and took a new line across a zigzag, thus forming the triangle, and also made a new gravel-surfaced area at the top for parking and turning. The Planning Service requested a retrospective planning application. This was later submitted, and the estate took advice from SNH on reseeding and other reinstatement, mainly involving boulders. The Planning Service recommended retrospective consent, with conditions on the reseeding and reinstatement, which the estate had agreed to do.

At the Marr Committee meeting of Aberdeenshire Council on 13 December 2005, one Councillor proposed refusal, and was seconded. However, the Committee allowed permission by a majority vote. This was inconsistent, for the Committee had just rejected unanimously the officer's recommendation for permission for a retrospective application by Invercauld Estate at Gleann an t-Slugain. The arguments of Councillor Luffman against the Slugain track applied equally to the Dinnet one, yet he opposed the Slugain one but agreed to the Dinnet one.

34. Upgrading and widening on Morven, Dinnet Estate, early summer 2004

A large excavator was used on an existing track east of Morven Lodge, within the Cairngorms National Park, to connect with upgraded tracks and new tracks (33. above) on the east side of Culblean. Although this was an engineering operation involving substantial widening and new spoil heaps, the estate did the work without seeking planning consent. The total length affected was about 5 km.

35. Upgrading of Fungle south of Ballochan, Forest of Birse, early winter 2005

This was an existing track. In 2005, the Birse Community Trust commissioned Upper Deeside Access Trust to oversee excavator works to upgrade the track surface and drains. Dr David Jenkins was concerned when he saw the works, and asked if I could pay a visit. Though not the landowner, BCT holds certain commonty rights, and the landowner agreed to the track upgrading, which would obviously ease access by the estate for shooting and management such as muirburn. I visited the track in December 2005 and wrote a report which is in an Appendix below.

After my report went to UDAT, John Addy of BCT wished to visit the track with me and Andrew Coleman of UDAT, and I suggested that Sandy Walker be invited. In June 2006 we all went together to view the works. The aim was to discuss lessons for future works, and suggest improvements that should be made on reinstatement and on certain measures to reduce the risks of erosion and other problems. As well as viewing the track and drains, we walked beyond the end of the track to inspect the path repairs, all the way to beyond the Glen Esk march. The site visit was successful, and the main recommendations made by Mr Walker and myself were accepted. Repair works were to be put in hand.

36. Invermark Estate, Glen Esk, Angus

The date is uncertain, but since the mid 1980s one track has appeared for 3 km from south-west of Dalbrack to the top of the Black Hill, and a 0.3 km fork is near White Cairn north of the Baillies by Tarfside. These are mostly wheel tracks, with some excavation on wet peaty ground towards Black Hill.

37. Millden Estate, Glen Esk, Angus

A new owner came in 2005, financier Richard Hanson in Doughty Hanson & Co at Pall Mall, London, involved in asset management across Europe, and according to information on the internet he is worth £90 million. In 2005 I noticed a new wheel track from Keddloch going north up the Red Shank to Hill of Cat and then east, for a total of 5.3 km during erection of an electrified deer-fence round the Millden march. A new excavated track was constructed in late 2008 or spring 2009 for 1 km to Hill of Saughs near Mount Battock, on the line of a former wheel track. About the same time, a new 1.2-km track extended from west of the Burn of Turret up Allrey and along the flat top, and in June 2010 a local resident told me that this continued for 1 km past Castle Hill to Bennygray. South of the river North Esk on 4 June 2010 I saw 17.4 km of new tracks and also 10.7 km of former tracks plus 0.7 km of former wheel tracks resurfaced with gravel, and 1.8 km of new wheel tracks, including from Keenie to west of Corharncross on a section where an excavator was working. Other tracks went up the north sides of Burn of Ranoch and Burn of Holmhead, and on Craig of Dalhastnie, Bulg, Broom Craig, West Wirren, Black Craig, Clash of Wirren and East Knock. Several of the new tracks cross grass fields. In the catchment of Burn of Turret, on the north side of the North Esk, I saw totals of 4.8 km of new tracks and 14.2 km of former tracks resurfaced with gravel up Grteen Burn and on Hill of Turret, Burn of Turret, Millstone Craig, Black Craig, Wester Cairn, Allrey and Mount Een. Also there are new wheel tracks for 0.3 km on Hill of Saughs, 1.2 km to the summit of Mount Battock, and a wheel track on a former path on lower Green Burn. Within the catchment of Glen Tennet were 5.6 km of new tracks and 2.9 km of former tracks resurfaced with gravel, on Mount Een, Brown's Towers, Craig Soales, Hill of Cat, Glencat, Burn of Keddloch, up the ridge south-west of Mudlee Bracks to its summit and continuing east past Hill of Cammie to end north-west of Loch Tennet at 535856. All new tracks and resurfaced tracks were surfaced with gravel from borrow pits or from the line of the road. Large boulders were excavated from rocky sections and deposited on vegetation at the side. The boulders are pale and obvious from afar, but most sections had few or none. According to local information, further construction is likely. The total comes to 36.9 km of new tracks and 43.9 km of former tracks surfaced with gravel, plus 0.4 of wheel track on a former footpath, grand total 81.2 km.

38. New track on Glendye Estate near Banchory, May 2008 and April 2010

A large excavator was used to make a new track for 7 km up the south side of Water of Aven, without a planning application. Work began in early December 2007 at 625890 from an existing track that came from the plantation on to Hill of Westerburn. The new track went north along the west side of the fenced plantation to 627899, next north-west to the Water of Aven at 625900, and then westwards along the south side of the Water of Aven. Contractors worked during the months of winter and spring, until the Council issued a stop notice in June. By then, the track had continued west to 583878.

Glacial till includes a high content of clay and silt, so pollution of the stream with silt was inevitable. Such deposition requires a licence from SEPA, but the estate did not apply for it or notify SEPA. The River Dee is a European Union SAC (Special Area of Conservation) and hence of international importance, and the SAC covers not just the Dee but its main tributaries including Water of Aven. SNH should have been notified, but the estate ignored this also. At one section, the driver crossed a steep slope above the stream, cutting a vertical face into glacial till on the uphill side, and dumping fill on the downhill side. This buried vegetation on the downhill side and much fill went into the Water of Aven, including boulders and subsoil. The new slope is so steep and unstable that further run-off and erosion due to rain and frost are certain.

The driver could have removed the cut material and taken it to the nearest borrow pit. This would have prevented burial of vegetation on the downhill side and greatly reduced silt pollution of the water. The tall heather would have acted as a trap to hold smaller amounts of silt washed off the track edge and on to the downhill side. Removal of downhill spoil should be a requirement of reinstatement.

These observations and photographs were sent to the Planning Department of Aberdeenshire Council, and John Forster, other individuals and the North East Mountain Trust objected to the Council. After a site visit and contact with the developers, Planning Inspector Iain Alley wrote on 4 June to Mr Forster, stating that the developers had been required to cease operations until the planning issues can be lawfully decided. The estate claimed that the track did not require planning consent because it was for agriculture. Council planners decided against enforcement, on the grounds that the case was uncertain because of the claim on agriculture.

This track penetrated far into previously trackless moorland used by specially protected birds such as merlin and golden eagle. There is a serious risk of adverse effects on the birds from the work itself and the increased use of the track that ensues.

The North East Mountain Trust condemned the estate for these unauthorised works. Jennifer Cook, chairwoman of NEMT, stated 'We call upon Aberdeenshire Council staff and councillors to stop further works, urgently. They should take enforcement action, requiring the estate to remove the works and to reinstate disturbed ground completely. SEPA and SNH must support the Council by serving their own enforcement procedures. And it is high time that the Scottish Government and its Planners set far higher standards for developments in Scotland's hill glens.'

In November 2007, the Public Inquiry Reporters' Unit in Falkirk concluded an appeal. Invercauld Estate had excavated a widened track from Balmore to Auchtavan, Aberdeenshire Council served an enforcement notice, and the estate appealed. The estate's excuse was that the works were for agriculture, but the Reporter nevertheless concluded that the works should have required planning permission. It follows that the unwillingness of Aberdeenshire planning staff to take firm action against Glendye Estate on the grounds that the Aven track might be for agriculture and so a stop notice might lead to adverse legal consequences for the Council, is without foundation or precedent. It is an example of inconsistent prevarication shown by planning staff over the Old Military Road at Corgarff, several (not just one) track in Gleann an t-Slugain, and several (not just one) track at Culblean on Dinnet Estate.

Since the above was written, Glendye Estate has carried out remedial works on the track and SEPA has reviewed and approved these. Enforcement via removal of subsidy is being considered by the cross-compliance unit in the Scottish Government's Rural Payments and Inspections Directorate.

Despite the stop notice, in late April 2010 the estate extended the track for another 0.5 km west to the Tomanarrach Burn, where the excavator driver cut the banks to allow a crossing. As in the earlier section, the excavator cut into a steep slope of glacial till above the Water of Aven, depositing much cut material on the downhill side and leaving a steep bank on the uphill side. This caused movement of boulders and subsoil, including silt and clay, to fall into the stream, and the bank is so steep and unstable that further additions of subsoil with silt are certain. No attempt was made to save the extant vegetation and topsoil, which were destroyed by burial.

39. Socach near Cushnie, Aberdeenshire

In August 2008, about 100 m of an existing wheel track was excavated at 481095. The excavator removed the strip between the wheel tracks, dumping some material on vegetation at the side, and the rest on to dips in the track. The result will be prone to erosion. No attempt was made to reinstate excavated vegetation and topsoil, or prevent extant vegetation from being buried.

40. Dinnet Estate, Lary Hill

In August 2008, an excavator was used at the col between Lary Hill and Tom Liath to upgrade an existing track from Morven Lodge to Glen Fenzie, at 334027. The work was similar to that in 38 above, with omission of reinstatement.

41. Finzean Estate

A new track was excavated for about 1 km on the south side of Peter Hill, from 575881 eastwards to 584881. The exact date of the works is uncertain, but a local resident recalls it as about November 2004.

42. Delachuper, Candacraig Estate, Aberdeenshire

In early summer 2009 the estate excavated a new track for 300 m uphill from this house, without a planning application. No attempt was made to retain vegetation or topsoil, and gravel banks were left in an unstable condition. A local resident informed the Cairngorms National Park Authority, whereupon the recently appointed CNPA enforcement officer, former Councillor Bruce Luffman, made a site visit and contacted the estate. Following this, at the end of June the estate covered the exposed gravel banks with earth.

43. Kerloch, Strachan

Three tracks for grouse-shooting were excavated since the mid 1980s. One starting on low moorland south of Midtown runs 0.5 km to Blarourie top, and a nearby one goes for 1 km to cross Black Burn and then heads west. The third track is an extension from an existing track round the south side of Kerloch summit. It heads north-east for 300 m, followed by wheel tracks for 200 m to the summit and with considerable erosion on the last section.

44. Lecht Ski Centre

Since the late 1980s, the Lecht Ski Company made tracks so that staff could drive vehicles to ski lifts on the south (Aberdeenshire) side and the north (Morayshire) side. The company made about 2 km of tracks by depositing hardcore and gravel on thick peat. The track uphill south of Osprey ski-tow later became used also for passengers riding Deval Karts. During the 2000s the company excavated new tracks for mountain-biking on the Moray side, too narrow for a vehicle apart from a narrow one such as an Argocat. The tracks zigzag so much that it is hard to estimate total length, but at least 2 km. They can be viewed on the Lecht website. Cut and fill banks were left steep, especially the former, and became unstable due to movement in frost, rain and groundwater. Although the area of turf excavated from the line of the track far exceeded the area of cut and fill, much bare ground was left, leading to further erosion, and boulders that rolled downhill remained lying on top of vegetation.

45. Glen Avon Estate, Tomintoul

In 2009 a new track was excavated from 155068 for 300 m east along the river bank towards the exit of Burn of Loin. The NEMT notified Moray Council and the Cairngorms National Park Authority. The former took no action, but the CNPA wrote to the estate, requesting a retrospective planning application. This is within the Cairngorm Mountains NSA.

46. Mar Lodge Estate, Braemar

Wheel tracks go from the old track from Claybokie to upper Glen Quoich for 0.7 km east on to the plateau of Creag Bhalg, starting a short distance north of the deer fence that encloses the south side of Creag Bhalg. To judge from the vegetation on the tracks, they were made in the late 1980s or early 1990s, perhaps during the ownership of John Kluge. This is within the Deeside and Lochnagar NSA.

47. Glen Avon Estate, Tomintoul
Since 2000, a bulldozed track has been made from Faindouran Lodge north up the ridge towards Cnap an Dobhrain for about 400 m., made in 2009 or 2010. This is within the Cairngorm Mountains NSA.

48. Colly Rigs south-west of Lumphanan
In the 2000s, a crude track was excavated from the farm Nether Tillylair, heading west through pinewood and bichwood south of a fence to a col at 532029. From 537028 on that track, another was made south-west to 535024 near a small hilltop north of Mortlich. The two totalled 1.6 km. In late summer 2010 a new track was excavated along the west side of the triangle, SSE from 532029 to 535024 for 0.5 km. During work on both tracks, many pines were uprooted and left where they fell. No attempt was made to retain turf and upper soil horizons, thus destroying ground vegetation along the lines of the tracks, no drains had been made, and many boulders and much subsoil had been deposited on surface vegetation.

49. Raebush, Dinnet Estate
At least 4 km of wheel tracks have occurred since 1982 on the moor south of Raebush and west of the public road from Loch Davan.

50. Sron nan Gabhar near Auchallater, Invercauld Estate
A wheel track has appeared since 1994 for 1.8 km from Sron Dubh to Sron nan Gabhar.

51. Glas Tulaichean, Invercauld Estate
A wheel track has appeared since 1994, starting north-west of Glenlochsie Lodge and running up Breac-reidh to a cairn just west of Glas Tulaichean summit. It continues WSW to a hilltop west of Faire Ghlinne Mhoir and then turns south to a point west of Clais Odhar. From the cairn noted above, another track runs south-east to 055755 where it forks. The west fork heads downhill SSE and then 061745 turns south to end downhill at 061734. The other fork goes south-east past a hilltop at 824 m and then south to a col at 792 m. These wheel tracks combined total 11.6 km.

52. Corndavon, Gairnshiel and Home beats, Invercauld Estate
Since 1994, new wheel tracks have been made for 1.5 km south-west of Corndavon Lodge on the west side of the Easter Kirn burn, 0.5 km east of the Lodge on to the Black Hillock, a total of 1.5 km for a track on Tom Odhar and one nearby on Tom a' Chatha above Easter Sleach, 0.2 km on Moine Bhuidhe at Glas-choille, 0.3 km north of Culardoch, 0.6 km to Bad nan Dearcag up Glen Feardar, and new excavated tracks totalling 1.5 km on the lower partly-wooded slopes of Little Elrick north of Alltdourie near Invercauld House.

53. Delnadamph Estate, Strathdon
New wheel tracks have been made since the mid 1980s for 0.6 km on Tom Dunan, 1.0 on Little Geal Charn, 1.4 km on Carn Oighreag, 0.2 at Easgach, 0.6 km at Coire Dhomhain, and 0.5 km at Carn Ealasaid, totalling 3.7 km.

54. Candacraig Estate, Strathdon
Since the mid 1990s, wheel tracks have been made for 1.9 km on Camock Hill and 1.3 km on Little Scraulac, total 3.2 km.

55. Allargue Estate, Strathdon
Extra wheel tracks have been made since the mid 1990s for 2.3 km on Carn Ealasaid.

56. Tillypronie Estate, Strathdon
Since the mid 1980s, a wheel track has appeared at Preas Whin for 0.4 km.

57. Dinnet Estate

A new wheel track for 0.4 km has been made since the 1980s at the lower part of Rashy Burn, mostly on its west side, and two longer wheel tracks totalling 3.1 km north of the summit of Culblean Hill, the longer one down the west side of the burn towards Redburn and the shorter one further west from 404014 curving southwards round to 402010.

58. Glen Avon Estate, Tomintoul

Since the mid 1980s, a wheel track has occurred for 0.3 km on Cnap Chaochan Aitinn.

59. Cabrach Estate

New wheel tracks totalling 7.1 km have appeared on this estate since the mid 1990s. These are up Allt na Craoibhe-caorainn, up the burn south-west of Cairnbrallan, along Scors Burn, Rounamuck Hill, west of Gauch, Corse of Garbet, and including 1.3 km from Kindy Burn east to the summit of The Buck.

60. Glendye Estate, Banchory

Since the late 1980s, probably since the late 1990s, a new wheel track has been made for 1.1 km to the summit of Mount Battock, linking with one made from Millden Estate in Glen Esk.

61. Invermark Estate, Glen Esk

Since the late 1980s, wheel tracks totalling 3.4 km have been made, the main one from north of the Baillies to the col north-west of Craig Brawlin, the shorter one for 0.6 km from the Hill of Saughs running east downhill south of the Burn of Adekimore, with a short 0.2 km fork at the east end.

62. Dinnet Estate, Culblean

On 12 April 2011 I saw a new track which I had not seen there on 3 April 2009. Starting on the line of 0.6 km of wheel track, it continues west for 0.8 km of new track along the north side of the 604-m summit east of Culsten Burn, almost on the crest and summit, and for some distance along the exposed freely drained ridge further west. I did not walk to the track but viewed it in good sunlight with binoculars. It appears to be well made, by depositing gravel from borrow-pits on top of the heather, not excavating along the entire length of the track as has been typical of most new tracks in northern Scotland in the past.

Chapter 5. Controversial new hill tracks outside north-east Scotland

The list below includes cases since 1982. Aitken (1995) summarised some earlier ones at Allt Mhoille on Ben Cruachan, Camasunary near Loch Coruisk, and Gleann Lichd on the Kintail Estate of the National Trust for Scotland, and a track to an aerial at Drumochter Pass in the Drumochter Hills SSSI. Also he emphasised the rapidly increasing damage to hill vegetation, soils and landscape from all-terrain vehicles in recent years travelling off prepared tracks, especially on peaty soils.

1. Comer, Ben Lomond, Stirling District, 1982

In 1982, farmer Anthony Ferguson bulldozed a 5-km track from Comer at 386040 at the top of old fields in Gleann Dubh, on the Aberfoyle side of Ben Lomond, over the hill to Cailness at 343063 on the shore of Loch Lomond (*The Scotsman*, August 22 1983), to gain easy access to a house on Loch Lomond, though ostensibly also for agriculture. Because the route for about 2 km lay above 300 m within a NSA, it required planning approval and referral to the CCS. The CCS did not object, and Stirling District Council then gave planning approval. The construction was crudely done by bulldozing, leaving conspicuous scars on a zigzag line down the steep hillside above Cailness. Stirling planners were displeased with the work done, which the Friends of Loch Lomond called "a visual obscenity".

The Council applied to Secretary of State George Younger for an Article 4 Direction to prevent the farmer from bulldozing further tracks, but the Secretary of State in 1973 decided to refuse these powers. As usual, the Scottish Office backed traditional local land interests at the expense of wider national ones. Stirling District Council's Director of Planning Maurice Dobson responded, 'From now on it appears that councils will be powerless to stop tracks like this criss-crossing the most sensitive areas in Scotland'. However, the widespread publicity about the Comer case was the trigger to removing the altitude limit in NSAs. Subsequently and in consequence, planning approval for a new vehicle track became necessary anywhere in a NSA, not just above 300 m.

2. Gualin Estate, Durness, Sutherland, 1987

In 1987 the syndicate absentee proprietors of Gualin Estate applied for planning permission to build a vehicle track for Argocats from Gualin Lodge for 12 km up Strath Dionard to Loch Dionard, with a 1-km spur northwards along the banks of the River Dionard, inside a NSA and a NNR (Baldwin 1987). The proposed 12-km route followed the line of a former footpath. The Nature Reserve Agreement, signed before the 1981 Wildlife & Countryside Act, did not prohibit all-terrain vehicles. Such use in SSSI and NNR agreements after the Act would have included this as a potentially damaging operation.

NCC did not object, on the grounds that a track would reduce damage by Argocats crossing peat while carrying anglers. This had caused severe impacts to vegetation, peat and pools. Thompson & Thompson (1991) attributed a decline of greenshank pairs to these impacts. They had noted an absence of greenshank on the most affected sites, which had been occupied in years before the more recent severe impacts.

NCC offered a big sum to pay most of the construction costs. NCC had already been paying a reported £12 000 per year to the owners, to compensate for alleged losses incurred through letting of fishing where access was on foot and not by vehicle. Nevertheless the owners continued to use Argocats for their personal use to reach the fishing. Ironically, NCC could have bought the estate in 1981, after the death of former owner Marjorie Fergusson, for a small fraction of the total paid for compensation plus grant-aid for track construction. Even in Mrs Fergusson's time, the occasional use of tracked vehicles to the loch had churned vegetation and peat, though to a lesser extent than the frequent use of all-terrain vehicles by later owners.

The CCS opposed the application to construct a vehicle track, as did a number of organisations and individuals. The CCS stated that 'the construction of a track would be an irreversible diminution of wilderness character, whereas pressure of public opinion might eventually lead to a reversion to the earlier practice of fishermen walking to the loch, coupled with a cessation or reduction in use of all-terrain vehicles' (CCS 1988, p.12). Because of the CCS objection,

Boulders from new track by Mar Estate rolled on to 1800s Glen Ey track; new track beyond on east side of glen, October 1986.

Track by Mar Estate on east side of Glen Ey, short section on right gives access for shooting; did not require planning approval because said to be part of a forestry grant scheme, though almost all outside the wood, May 1981.

the application had to be notified to the Secretary of State. It was eventually approved in July 1988. The controversy was described in other publications (*BBC Wildlife* 1987, 5, 306–307, and January 1988, p. 37; and *Rambling Today*, autumn 1991, 17–18).

3. Letterewe & Fisherfield Estate, Little Gruinard, Wester Ross, 1990

Serious conflict arose when Letterewe & Fisherfield Estate, owned by Dutch businessman Paul Fentener van Vlissingen, applied for planning permission to construct a 4.5-km track for land rovers far up the west side of the Little Gruinard River, in a formerly trackless glen inside the Wester Ross NSA. The application stated that the track was intended for crofter David Mackenzie to gain easier access to his sheep (*Press & Journal*, February 27, 1992). Previously, he had taken feed on an Argocat. The CCS, the Association for the Protection of Rural Scotland, the Ramblers' Association, and a number of other organisations and individuals objected. This led to a Public Inquiry in 1992.

As stated in David Morris's Inquiry precognition on behalf of the Scottish Council of the Ramblers' Association, 'the use of an Argocat to deposit winter feed is causing some impact on vegetation and soils. This is, however, relatively limited in extent and in many places it is difficult to identify the route taken by the Argocat. It is wrong to suggest that the present use of the Argocat is causing unsightly scars and to imply that there would be less impact from a constructed hill track....The proposed construction of a hill track from Little Gruinard to Fionn Loch, as described in planning application RC/1990/930, would significantly damage the wild-land qualities of the Wester Ross National Scenic Area. It would create a serious intrusion of a built facility into a tract of relatively natural terrain.' It should be noted that this area, lying on the large tract of hill land between Loch Maree and Loch Broom, was proposed as one of four National Parks for Scotland in the CCS's 1991 report *The Mountain Areas of Scotland*. Most of the glen up Little Gruinard River fell within the area zoned by the CCS as the 'Mountain core', where the strictest protection should prevail.

The Scottish Office's Reporter to the Public Inquiry found in favour of the planning application, again manifesting the Scottish Office's bias towards traditional local land interests at the expense of general national interests. Highland Regional Council's planning officials set inadequate conditions on the approval, so the construction in 1994 caused severe impacts to ground and landscape. The crofter's grazing lease had only two years left to its termination.

During meetings leading to 'The Letterewe Accord', which I attended as a technical advisor to the Ramblers' Association, representatives of mountaineering and rambling bodies voiced suspicion that the track's purpose was for the estate to gain easy vehicle access for fishing and shooting. The estate denied this. However, clearly evident at the Accord meetings was the keenness of the estate owner, his partner and his gamekeepers to have this track, and their surprisingly aggressive statements about objectors including the CCS. They were especially hostile to CCS chairman Roger Carr. The owner and his partner had been involved in opposing the CCS proposal for a National Park in the area, and showed this at a public meeting organised by CCS and attended by Mr Carr. The owner's partner asserted at one of the Accord meetings that Carr had got his own back by persuading the CCS to object to the track. Having been a commissioner on the CCS board, I rejected her claim. An impartial observer would find it hard to understand why the estate went to such lengths to make conditions slightly easier for a crofter who had hitherto fed his sheep without difficulty. It would be interesting to find how often the crofter used the track for feeding sheep, compared with the estate for fishing and shooting. The proposal conflicted with Mr van Vlissingen's publicly expressed sentiments favouring wilderness (e.g. in the *Newsletter of the Association for the Protection of Rural Scotland*, autumn 1991).

4. Pitmain Estate, Kingussie, 1992

In 1991, Highland Regional Council approved a new vehicle track proposed by Pitmain Estate, despite objections from several voluntary conservation groups and a CCS recommendation to the Council to refuse consent. In summer 1992, Pitmain Estate bulldozed the track in the Monadh Liath above Kingussie, Inverness-shire, on land then owned by Mr Lucas Aardenburg from the Netherlands. The track was constructed for 2 km from a point west of 718075 on the west side of Carn an Fhreiceadain to a lunch hut at 719094 in the headwaters of the River Dulnain, an area that had previously been road-less. Some local people opposed it, including Kingussie chemist John Allen, leader of the local

Gully caused by water flowing from track, Peter Hill, Finzean Estate, October 1984.

Track on Ord Ban, Rothiemurchus Estate, for 'land rover event', September 1998.

Track for land rover event in native pine-wood Site of Special Scientific Interest, Rothiemurchus, following earlier track by machine carrying cut trees, September 1998.

mountain rescue team. He was reported (*Sunday Telegraph*, August 9) stating that such tracks 'completely destroy the wilderness quality of an area. Soon there will be no areas where one cannot drive, and no wild land'.

OS maps in 1928 and 1933 show a track from Pitmain Lodge up Allt Mor to a hut below Bad Each. I do not know the date of the extension on to the west side of Carn an Fhreiceadain, but aerial photographs show evidence of upgrading by 1961, along the line of an existing vehicle track. The track ended at 717075, and wheel tracks on freely-drained ground continued for 400 m downstream and across a small ford.

Approving the new track, the Council accepted planning officer John Partridge's 'proposal to impose two "onerous but entirely necessary" planning conditions requiring the immediate blending of cuttings and fillings into the natural contours of the hill, and the reseeding of exposed soil in the first growing season' (*Strathspey & Badenoch Herald*, October 10 1991). The newspaper continued 'Nevertheless, Councillor Major Nigel Graham, while not pressing the issue to a vote, expressed concern over the visual intrusion of the road and suggested a way in which the planning authority could ensure reinstatement of hillsides where such conditions were not met. "I see hills all over the country with these ghastly scars on them. Personally, I think we should be taking a bond on this, and a very considerable one"'. However, the Council did not resolve to make a bond necessary.

Planning conditions followed recommendations in the CCS (1987) *Environmental Design and Management of Ski Areas in Scotland: A Practical Handbook*. When the estate bulldozed the track, it used a different alignment from that in the application and largely ignored the conditions in the approval. The cut banks were too high (up to 4 m) and too steep (up to 45° gradient), and so unstable and poor for plant colonisation (30–35° or less is stable). Inspection showed no sign of reseeding.

5. Mrs Cameron Estate, south side of Loch Lyon, Perthshire, c1997

This vehicle track was bulldozed for around 6 km on the south side of Loch Lyon around 1997–98, on acquisition of the estate by John Cameron of Glen Lochay in his wife's name. Although an SSSI ran down to the loch shore, SNH did not object to this track. SNH officer Stuart Pritchard at Battleby told the MC of S that he could do nothing to stop it and that the scientific interest lay above the proposed track. The track is reputed by walkers to have been made insensitively. Later the estate proposed extending it into Glen Lochay over the shoulder of Beinn Heasgarnich to a high altitude. SNH objected because the line would cross a priority habitat in a *Natura* site. Since then the matter is apparently now in abeyance.

The first 100 m of the lower track re-used the existing sward. The contractor, McLarty of Crieff, has done work of this kind for SNH, mainly on footpath construction. The method, involving re-use of the sward, derived from early experience in constructing a section of West Highland Way through Crianlarich Forest. On that section, the operator did a good job along a forest ride underlain by poorly drained peaty soils. He formed a new surface with freely drained gravel, then moved back to lift the sward from the next (ahead) section, and placed it forward on to that piece of track which had already been constructed. He excavated turves with a back-actor bucket and placed them carefully, knuckling them down to good effect.

Subsequently the turves settled. This worked particularly well in the plantation, where much of the vegetation was rank and hung over the narrow spaces between excavated turves, concealing these spaces while the ground settled. This method has also been used on heavily grazed ground, but less successfully, and to bring it up to the standard of the Crianlarich section would require much hand work. Nevertheless, the result was far more satisfactory than in the usual past cases where the operator wasted valuable vegetation and topsoil, destroying them by careless burial under subsoil spoil. Obviously, individual slabs of sward cannot be laid in exact fit. However, a skilled excavator driver can do a good job if given guidance on the aims.

6. Forest Enterprise, Ard Trilleachan, Loch Etive, winter 1997–98

Mike Newbury of the Mountaineering Council of Scotland has contributed a separate account of this track (Appendix). The OS 1 inch to the mile maps of 1947 and 1956 show a road ending at the Bonawe quarries at Loch Etive's south end. At the loch head, a road ran a short way from Gualachulain to a pier. Between these road-ends stretched a road-less slope for miles, penetrated only by a footpath beside the shore.

Stuart Rae stands on track for land rover event beside River Luineag, Rothiemurchus, pile of excavated soil dumped, September 1998.

Track by Glendye Estate at lower Water of Aven, near-vertical bank above, steep fill bank with excavated boulders and heather turf and gravel, most vegetation destroyed, 8 May 2008.

7. Forest Enterprise, Ben Venue, Perthshire, 2001–02

FE made a vehicle track on the hill's south side, coinciding with the line of a footpath for 1 km, to ease access for extracting shot deer. Mike Newbury and Mike Dales of the MC of S inspected it in May 2002, finding the same serious flaws as in the Loch Etive track (above). Following complaints by the MC of S, the FE implemented works to reduce the gradients of cut and fill slopes, install adequate cross-drains, construct stone fords at burn crossings, even out the heaps of turf, spoil and stones, and re-seed bare ground. Also, FE's landscape architects produced a 'Forest Management Guideline' on 'Design and Construction of Access Tracks'. Newbury (2002) gave more detail in his article 'Healing hill tracks: success!' in *The Scottish Mountaineer*, number 12, p. 36.

Ben Venue was in one of the most scenically valuable parts of the Trossachs, and in the centre of the Queen Elizabeth Forest Park and the area agreed for Loch Lomond & Trossachs National Park, and now within that newly formed Park. It may be wondered why FE should be in charge of such poorly constructed tracks in such outstanding areas as Loch Etive and Ben Venue. However, FE's own forest roads and also the private forest roads approved by the Forestry Commission involve no attempt to reduce over-steepened gradients of cut or fill slopes, or to save vegetation or topsoil and replace them in correct order so as to maximise reinstatement.

8. Sallachy Estate, Lairg, Sutherland, 2008–09

The estate made a 3.9-km track without planning consent, despite the land being designated SSSI, SAC and SPA. SNH objected. Highland Council requested the estate to remove the track and reinstate the ground. The estate appealed but lost the decision in March 2009, www.dpea.scotland.gov.uk, ref. Highland (08-00131-FULSU).

9. Corriegarth Estate, Gorthleck, Stratherrick 2009

The *Press & Journal* (Highland edition) of 14 August 2009 carried a report by Iain Ramage that 'Highland Council officials have urged the Scottish Government to review laws which currently allow landowners to bypass the planning system when building roads across mountains they own. The move was prompted after a vehicle track was carved out of a hillside'. 'This prompted protests to the council and from local people who believe their prominent and well-loved landmark 2,600ft Beinn Bhuraich has been vandalised. But the authority is helpless because the road was built under "permitted development rights", which means the landowner does not require planning permission. The route in this case connects two areas of hill grazing for hill farming which are separated by another laird's estate. Confirming that a number of people had raised concerns about the track, senior council planner Richard Hartland said: "We also expressed concern about the opportunity for estates to drive tracks under 'permitted development rights' and have lobbied Scottish ministers to bring such works within planning control. We have investigated it at length and the objectors have asked us to bring these matters to the Scottish Government's attention". The estate is owned by Andrew Fraser. The track runs for 4 km on to the 780-m Beinn Bhuraich from Carn Liath east of Loch Mhor. A photograph of it with an excavator is on p. 6 of an article by Calum Brown (2010) and another photograph on the magazine's front cover.

A complaint about the track by a constituent of Peter Peacock MSP induced him to start a petition against such unregulated tracks (Peacock 2010). At a debate in the Scottish Parliament on 9 June 2010, he received cross-party support. In response, Transport Minister Stewart Stevenson stated that by law, any track of over 1 km requires an environmental impact assessment (EIA) and that the government will review the Permitted Development Order. However, he did not say what action he would take if an applicant fails to produce an EIA, or when the review would occur. Also, although a new track for wind turbines or a telecommunications mast is stated to require an EIA, this appears not to apply to Permitted Development involving agriculture, forestry or repair to an existing track. The Minister therefore gave an unclear statement.

Later, he stated that the General Permitted Development order, which allows tracks for agriculture and forestry to be exempt from planning regulations, will be reviewed in 2010. This the government has failed to do (McNeish 2011). The government in 2011 stated that a review has been authorised and will be go for consultation. This removed the subject from being decided until after the Scottish Parliament election in May.

Hebe Carus (2011) of the MC of S published a brief article in February bringing news on the political events up to date. In a Parliamentary Debate, "….the Minister responsible, Stewart Stevenson, is on record saying he would come back with his further thoughts soon after the summer recess. This had still not happened by October, so I again pursued the subject. In response to this a letter was received from the Minister (on the A & C News pages of the website) stating there would be a consultation to gauge the relevance of the 2007 Heriot Watt University report (commissioned by the then Scottish Executive) which gave clear recommendations to bring hill tracks under planning control, which sadly sounds like it is being kicked into the long grass. This is of course complicated by the fact the Minister stepped down in December due to the travel/snow debacle and the election in May. I will continue to pursue this matter, but if you feel strongly about the damage that hill tracks are doing to our landscape and biodiversity, then continue to ask questions of your MSP, and the new Minister Keith Brown.

Chapter 6. Other new tracks in 2001–10 and others reported since 1990

1. West Monar, Wester Ross, July 2001 and 2002

A new vehicle track appeared in summer 2001 for 12 km from Bendronaig Lodge in the west (above Attadale on Loch Carron) to Pait Lodge in the east (on Loch Monar's south shore). It took the line of a former footpath (*The Angry Corrie* 2001, 51, p. 2, editorial note). In late July, Calum MacRoberts reported seeing bulldozers at Loch Calavie, and wrote to TAC 'They have stormed a trail through from Bendronaig Lodge to Pait....Another fine old path obliterated and now just a memory'. In late August, Christopher Horton saw 'the new and ugly bulldozed track which leads out to Pait Lodge'. Neither Highland Council nor SNH's local office knew of the track until informed by TAC and MC of S at the end of August (TAC editor). It is particularly obtrusive because a) it is by far the longest bulldozed track for land rovers and other wide vehicles (hence differing from the narrower, less obtrusive 12-km Argocat track in Strath Dionard), b) it has destroyed a footpath that fitted into the landscape, replacing it with a conspicuous landscape scar and a monotonous surface for walkers, c) it crosses one of the most remote and formerly road-less parts of the west Highlands, d) it is prominent from many long ridges and hilltops on higher ground.

In July 2002 the same estate destroyed another footpath by bulldozing a vehicle track for 3 km along the footpath line, from the 2001 road east of Bendronaig Lodge at 018392 to the burn of Allt a' Choire Sheasgaich at 027417. Comments b)–d) in the above paragraph apply again, and also the comment in a) above, about track width. Mike Dales, MCofS Access & Conservation Officer, reported (Dales 2002) that he had visited the site on 11 July, finding a large machine working on the line of a 30-cm wide footpath and turning it into a 3-m wide vehicle track.

His accompanying photograph shows a yet-untouched section of narrow footpath in excellent condition, and the obtrusive track immediately beyond the excavator. The photograph demonstrates clearly that the excavator operator made no attempt to save vegetation or topsoil and then replace them in reverse order. Also, he had deposited excavated boulders and subsoil in spoil heaps beside the track. Much of this had been dumped on top of plants. The excavator operator had left uphill banks too steep for stability, and drainage of the track surface was inadequate.

The MCofS reported these engineering operations to Highland Council on 18 July. HC planning officer John Greaves replied on 18 July, with reference to the estate, that the Council 'with their full cooperation have got their agreement to halt work immediately to allow time to review the position thoroughly'. Later, articles about this track appeared in *The Herald* and *The Times*. The MC of S was alarmed by the attitude shown by the estate as reported in the articles, especially comments attributed to owner Ewan Macpherson that the estate stopped the track work 'simply because it is the deer stalking season' and 'we intend to complete the operation next year'. In view of Mr Macpherson's comments, which do not agree with what Mr Greaves' letter of 18 July indicated, the MCofS wrote to Mr Greaves on 14 November, requesting again that Highland Council serve a Stop Order on estate, to prevent further work until the planning status is determined. Evidently the HC now regards the work as 'Permitted Development', not requiring planning approval.

2. Track extension at Carn na Lair, Reidhaven Estate, Inverness-shire, November 2001

This runs from 833234 at 490 m to 826237 at 580 m, near Carr Bridge. In a letter from Vice-convener Roy Turnbull, the Badenoch and Strathspey Conservation Group objected to the planning application because 'The proposed extension climbs c .90m altitude over a length of c 600m. This represents an average gradient of greater than 1 in 7, implying at this altitude and on an unsurfaced vehicle track, significant erosion problems....The intention is to continue up the spur which descends from Carn na Lair summit in an east–south-east direction, some 2 km west of the Slochd summit of the A9. It appears therefore that the track would be clearly visible in the middle distance for traffic travelling west for several km on the A9. The visibility of the track, some three metres wide and inclined towards the A9, would be increased by the erosion problem noted in 1, which would continuously expose fresh surfaces to view. The track would thereby represent a significant landscape scar to large numbers of people using the A9. The track represents a loss of wild land via the intrusion of a man made feature further into a semi-natural area.'

Track by Glendye Estate at upper Water of Aven, 25 April 2010.

'The area concerned lies within the Cairngorms Partnership Area, and both 2 and 3 above are contrary to the Cairngorms Partnership's *Vision for the future*. This states (p. 42 sect. 6) that there should be "a presumption against new hill vehicle tracks" and similarly (p. 43 sect. 10) "wherever possible the visual impact of roads on the landscape should be minimised". Indeed p. 42, sect. 6, suggests "the reinstatement of some hill tracks, particularly those that are highly visible, and those with associated erosion of surrounding land". Thus it appears to be the case that this track is precisely the kind of development that the Cairngorms Partnership's *Vision for the future* suggests should be removed, rather than be constructed.'

'The area of the proposed track also lies within Badenoch and Strathspey, and is therefore likely (with the support of Highland Council) to become part of the forthcoming Cairngorms National Park. National Planning Policy Guideline 14 - Natural Heritage - section 33 is therefore relevant. This states that "In the meantime*, planning authorities should take particular care to safeguard the landscape, flora and fauna of Loch Lomond and the Trossachs and the Cairngorms' (*i.e. until such time as the National Parks are established). This track would be one of the last images of the landscape of the Cairngorms National Park that people would carry with them as they continue their journey to the North."'

'It might also be added that Mar Lodge estate, owned by the National Trust, is restoring hill tracks whilst continuing commercial shooting activities, thus attracting clients who are prepared to enjoy the walk to their shoot. If one of the major attractions of the National Park is to be the quality of the walking that it offers, it is perhaps not unreasonable that this quality, and the principle of the long walk in, should be incorporated into all appropriate activities.'

'Finally, without prejudice to the present case, there would appear to be a need for a protocol to be developed for the construction of hill tracks on those rare occasions when it is considered appropriate. Many existing hill tracks have been constructed in such a manner that maximises their offence as an eyesore and a source of erosion, often by simply bulldozing a track across the land, with the material being pushed to one side in disorganised heaps.'

'Such a protocol, to be insisted upon by the planning authority, would involve the removal, and setting to one side, of the vegetation and soil/peat layers carefully, in large turves as thick as possible. These turves, along with any remaining organic material should then be used to cover any sub-soil, boulders and stony material by the side of the track. This would have the advantage of maximising the survival of vegetation and minimising the exposure of pale fresh granitic material, thus reducing problems of erosion and visibility.'

'Local experts in such matters have indicated to me a willingness to assist in the development of such a protocol with you should you wish to pursue this matter'.

The Planning Committee of Badenoch and Strathspey area of Highland Council (chairman Cllr Basil M.S. Dunlop), did not take up Mr Turnbull's offer, and approved the planning application in November 2001. Before this, in August, SNH agreed its report to ministers on the Cairngorms National Park, describing consultation and giving SNH's advice. In October, SNH published the report, with a map showing the area recommended by SNH for the National Park. The track route lies entirely within this area.

3. Alvie Estate, Inverness-shire

In 1998, two mobile phone masts and associated works were erected on the prominent spur of Creag a' Mhuilinn, some 2 km west of Loch Alvie. To service these installations, a 2-km vehicle road was built to the site from woods at Dalraddy near Allt Chriochain. Alvie Estate decided that no planning permission was required as the work involved upgrading an existing road which they claimed was indicated as such in early OS maps. Highland Council accepted this explanation, though reluctantly.

Inspection of the 1" and 6" maps based on the 1896 OS revision shows a track, marked as a double hatched line, up the face of An Sguabach and terminating at NH 834 101. However all OS maps produced subsequently have marked this only as a footpath. This original path can be faintly traced beyond Creag a' Mhuilinn (the antenna site) where it is scarcely discernible among the heather. The path width at this point is no more than 1.5 m. Therefore this was unlikely to have been anything more than a pony path which does not appear to have been used to any great extent recently, hence the almost intact heather cover.

The newly excavated track is now up to 3 m wide. Although it mainly follows the original path, it does divert from it in its lower section for about 400 m. This diversion is fairly steep and has been excavated out of the hillside, with little attempt at drainage. As a result, surface water now runs directly down the track surface and will inevitably cause further surface erosion and rills. In hard frost the road is virtually impassable to wheeled vehicles, due to the amount of ice lying on the surface.

Higher up, the track traverses the face of An Sguabach for about 1 km, where excavated subsoil spoil has been pushed over the edge with no attempt at re-instatement of the vegetation. This scar is now highly visible both to motorists on the A9 and to those walking in the Cairn Gorm area and other parts of the northern Cairngorms. There is also a further new visual intrusion of an overhead electricity supply line leading to the mast site. The site is outside the NSA boundary, but within the area recommended by SNH for the Cairngorms National Park.

4. Revack Estate, Inverness-shire

In July 2004, an excavator was used to widen a formerly narrow track starting at 084207 north of the bridge on the public road east of Dirdhu for 200 m, and then took the line of a former footpath north-east and then east for 2.6 km to link with the track south-west of Lyntelloch in Glen Lochy. This engineering operation was done without applying for planning permission, and left large spoil heaps with no attempt at reinstatement.

5. Callop, Glen Finnan

Colin Kinnear reported (The Scottish Mountaineer, Feb. 2008, Issue 38, p. 97) a new vehicle track being excavated on 28 October 2007 south of Callop, obliterating the former footpath up the glen along a right of way. The track ran for 200–300 yards, but he saw marker flags for most of the way to Allt Coire na Leacaich (i.e. more than 1 km from Callop), so he thought that the intention might be to extend the track to Glen Cona. His letter includes a photograph showing an excavator at the track-side. The cut banks on the uphill side were too steep for stability and the cut material had been placed flat along a width of about a metre along the downhill edge, leading below to a bank again too steep for stability. All excavated vegetation and topsoil had been destroyed by burial under subsoil and gravel from borrow pits, and there had been no reinstatement.

6. Allt Coire Fhar, Drumochter, Inverness-shire

In May 2008, a new excavated vehicle track was made for 4 km along the line of a footpath, destroying the path in the process. Beyond the top there stretches freely drained alpine vegetation, so vehicles will be able to go beyond, to the hilltops.

7–14. Other notable obtrusive tracks of unknown exact date, reported after 2001

Exact dates, though uncertain, were judged to be in the 6–10 years before 2001.

7. Alva Glen, Ochil Hills. A new track goes up the east side of the glen.

8. Extension to a track in Glen Kendrum west of Lochearnhead, Perthshire.

9. Long extension to a track up Glen Creran and Glen Ure, Argyll.

10. North of Balnain in Glen Urquhart, Inverness-shire, north beyond the old tracks.

11. North side of Loch Lyon, Perthshire, probably along 4.5 km of footpath, and then continuing on a new line for 2 km up Gleann Meran and then turning west into Gleann Cailliche between Beinn Mhanach and Beinn a' Chreachain for at least 1 km, made by John Cameron since 1998.

12. A track in Glen Lochay, Perthshire, made by farmer John Cameron.

13. From Loch Eil southwards on to the high north-east flank of Stob Coire a' Chearcaill for at least 2 km but the distance is not known exactly, seen in 2002.

14. A new track went up Gleann Sron a' Chreagain, probably along the line of a path up Abhainn Sron a' Chreagain, possibly 1.2 km, seen in 2002.

15. Coignafearn Estate, by Tomatin, Inverness-shire

In the late 1990s the estate was bought by Swedish lady Sigfrid Rausing of the family who founded Tetra Pak Company. Soon afterwards, the existing tracks were improved by re-profiling and by drainage works. A new track was made for 4 km from Dalbeg to 619145 on Allt Odhar, south-east of Carn na Saobhaidhe. There may be other new ones.

16. Dunmaglass Estate, Inverness-shire

Along the north-west side of the Monadh Liath, a new road went for about 5 km from Dunmaglass to a wind turbine on Carn Crom-gleann, and between 2002 and 2003 a new track was excavated from there for 3 km to 811-m Carn na Saobhaidhe, ending 30 m from the summit cairn. Also a branch for over 1 km ran to nearby 781-m Carn Mhic Iamhair to the east. This information came via David Jarman, from Hamish Johnston who commented that another 1.5 km of excavation between Allt Odhar and Carn na Saobhaidhhe would connect a track across hills from Strath Nairn to Strath Dearn.

Mr Johnston, of Macleod Road, Balloch, was reported in *The Strathspey & Badenoch Herald* (6 September 2006) saying that the track to Carn na Saobhaidhe 'was the largest, most crudely constructed and most inappropriate one he had come across during more than 30 years of hill walking.' 'The scarring of the landscape is made all the more offensive by the absence of any purpose'. The report went on to state that 'he wrote to Highland Council's director of planning, John Rennilson, who had confirmed that it was a permitted development.'

Mr Johnston was reported being unhappy about the track, because 'There is no farming up there'. In a recent article (Johnston 2006), he stated that in October 2004 he took measurements of the width of the track to Carn na Saobhaidhe, finding it a scar 10–12 m wide, including drains. The track itself spanned 8 m width, and the ditches on either side of 1.0–1.5 m width each. He observed, 'The track and ditches had been cut into the ground so that the road surface lies approximately 3 metres below the level of the surrounding land'.

The photograph shows that most of the track was excavated through thick peat down to the underlying stony parent material, and that no attempt was made to reinstate ground. Indeed, most of the excavated vegetation was buried under peat during the excavation, and much of the peat became buried under stony parent material that was excavated for ditches.

17. Loch Ossian to Loch Treig, Corrour Estates, Inverness-shire, summer 2006

The Corrour Estates, owned by Lisbet Rausing of the Swedish family who founded Tetra Pak Company (sister of the Coignafearn owner), excavated a vehicle track from the west end of Loch Ossian for 5.5 km to the south end of Loch Treig. An old pony path ran there, but the new works destroyed it. According to David Duncan of Kingussie, a former SNH officer with much experience of tracks, footpaths, and reinstatement, who visited at the end of August 2006 and in May 2008, the standard of work was low. The scarring is conspicuous from trains along the nearby railway as well as from further away. He was told that the upgraded track gave better access for vehicles so as to kill more deer, and that Highland Council planning department believed planning permission to be unnecessary. His photographs show that the excavator driver left the fill banks too steep and unstable, with bare subsoil and frequent cobbles on the surface, with no reinstatement of the cut or fill banks, and no reinstatement of borrow pits. Yet there must have been a massive excess of excavated vegetation and topsoil, now buried under subsoil. Even a small proportion of this could have been stored and utilised to reinstate all cut and fill banks, and all borrow pits.

18. Beinn na h-Iolaire near Tomatin, Inverness-shire

A track-wide firebreak was originally excavated on heather moorland just outside the eastern edge of a plantation, as far down as the south-east end of the wood, but later was turned into a new vehicle track leading to a telecommunications mast on the hilltop. The track is a conspicuous scar even at several miles' distance as one travels northwards by the A9 road or railway, due to imported pale material for the track surface.

19. Dalcheichart, Glen Moriston, Inverness-shire

This vehicle track was excavated about 1999, starting at the public road east of the former school at Dalcheichart, and heading north up morainic rocky moorland and then south-west, for a total of 1.3 km. In September 2006, a house was being built at the top of the first steep brae. The road gives access to a native woodland regeneration scheme, grant-aided by the Forestry Commission to a local builder who is landowner, with advice on woodland management by Scottish Woodlands. The road was well made, with no sign of erosion in September 2006. It is narrow, has been made with local material, and vegetation covers the banks almost completely, as well as some of the central line between vehicle wheels. A car can be driven on it.

20. Wind-farms

Many new roads have been made to wind-farms, such as Beinn Ghlas near Oban, Beinn an Tuirc in Kintyre, Novar in Easter Ross, Dunmaglass in Inverness-shire, Druim Derg in Perthshire, and on the Morayshire moors. This account excludes details on locations and lengths of these. Though conspicuous in the landscape, they are constructed with higher standards of running surfaces and drains than tracks for shooting, and are roads rather than tracks. Reinstatement has been better than on forestry or agricultural roads, but could readily have been increased with little or no extra effort.

21. Dalnaspidal Estate, Perthshire. May–July 2009

This was Dalnaspidal deer-forest, now taken over by Ben Alder Estate. David W. Duncan wrote 'I visited Dalnaspidal on Sunday 9 August 2009 to look at hill tracks constructed this year by the new owners of the Dalnaspidal Estate (also owners of Ben Alder and Coire Bhachdaidh and Camusericht). One track has been constructed along the east side of Loch Garry from Dalnaspidal Lodge for about 1 km and the other branches off south-east, running parallel to the railway for about 2.5 km, terminating at NN 666718. These tracks are designed to take 4 x 4 or high-clearance road vehicles. Beyond this termination a rough track has been built, crossing Allt Choire Leathanaidh and running for a further 1 km, but suitable only for hill vehicles such as Argocats. The new owners acquired Dalnaspidal estate with the objective of creating a driven grouse moor on the heathery hill of Sron na-Eiteich. The new tracks are seen as essential to improve accessibility for beaters and guns. The estate has also erected stock fencing and sheep-handling facilities to improve the management of the sheep flock, in an attempt to reduce the resident tick population. The Lodge itself is also undergoing renovation. Four workers (keepers and shepherds) are now employed on the estate.'

'The following are details of construction works to do with the tracks. A new bridge some 300 m south-east of the lodge is being constructed over the River Garry. This was incomplete at the time of the visit but is a substantial structure with concrete abutments and spanned with 12 m RSJs. The running surface of the tracks is between 3 m and 4 m in width, well cambered and with moderate gradients. In the few areas of thick peat the track has been floated over a layer of synthetic Terram. The surfacing and infill appear to have been won locally and most of the borrow pits have been re-profiled and re-turved. Excavated turves have been retained and replaced at the sides of the road over bare soil to minimise soil run-off and to lessen the impact on the landscape. This has not always been successful. On the steeper topside slopes there has been some slumping of material, which will probably lead to blocked culverts and consequent washouts. Piped culverts vary in diameter between 30 cm to 1 m and in some cases have been extended on the bottom side by 1 m or more to prevent water erosion of the track side. Splash stones have also been provided. A few passing places and two turning points have been constructed.'

'In general the construction has been of a reasonably high standard and a fair bit of attention has been paid to landscaping. By careful route-alignment and retention of vegetation, the tracks are not particularly visible from the A9 or railway, and as the vegetation grows they are likely to be less so in future years, but much will depend on regular maintenance of drainage to prevent blockages and washouts. Also the track which extends to the south-east is of much rougher construction, and, because it tackles steeper gradients, it may well erode in future and cause scarring.'

22. Glen Ogil Estate, Angus

In the late 1990s, financier John Dodd bought this estate, and since then rented shootings on neighbouring land of Careston estate at Nathro, and the shootings of Fern and of Glenquiech, as well as shootings on lands owned by the Earl of Airlie at Glen Moy and Rottal. Because all of this land lay outside the area of my 1981–82 survey and because I have seldom visited it since then, I have allocated fewer categories to the tracks. In some cases I was unsure whether a footpath on earlier maps was a narrow vehicle track, so I have lumped footpaths and former vehicle tracks under the heading of former tracks, when considering new excavated tracks on former tracks and the heading of wheel tracks on former tracks. Many tracks are certainly new and excavated, and these are conspicuous because of their recent construction, pale colour of gravel, and little or no vegetation on the track surfaces and banks. My study of the tracks relied on high-resolution satellite photographs in Google Earth from 2007 and fieldwork in mid August 2010 with Dave Windle and Derek Pyper. I knew the boundaries of the various estates previously.

On Glen Ogil estate with the small adjacent Glen Quiech combined there were 21.2 km of new tracks, mostly made in the last few years, and 7.5 km of wheel tracks. Some of the wheel tracks are certainly recent, but most might have been made before Mr Dodd came. On Nathro there were 12.0 km of new excavated tracks and 2.1 km of major upgrading of old tracks to the extent of being equivalent to a new track on a new line. On Fern there were 16.2 km of new tracks and 5.6 km of wheel tracks which may have been made before Mr Dodd came. On Rottal and Glen Moy there has been a major spread of tracks since 2003, mostly in the last few years. In the case of Rottal this amounted to 18.3 km of new tracks, 1.1 km of major upgrading, and 5.0 km of wheel tracks, some of which are recent. On Glen Moy the distances were 6.5 km of new tracks and 4.7 km of wheel tracks, some of which probably occurred before 2002. The grand totals were 73.8 km of new tracks, 3.2 km of major upgrading, and 17.2 km of wheel tracks.

According to a local informant, Mr Dodd paid a Kirriemuir contractor to do all the excavator work and the contractor was working on new tracks at Rottal after the August visit by Dave Windle, Derek Pyper and me. Hence the above figures may already be out of date and too low. It should be noted that some new tracks have been made continuously right through estate boundaries including fences, and thus connecting one estate with another. This is the case with Nathro and Glen Ogil, Fern and Glen Ogil, Glen Quiech and Glen Ogil, and Airlie and Glen Ogil.

Chapter 7. Problems facing planning officers

The main wave of new bulldozed and other hill track construction had passed before belated CCS action resulted in new regulations in 1980 within National Scenic Areas. Subsequently, smaller numbers of tracks appeared before the regulations became tightened further with a revision of The Town and Country Planning (General Permitted Development) (Scotland) Order 1992. This maintained the previous position that vehicle access tracks for agricultural and forestry operations were deemed to be Permitted Development (Clauses 18 and 22 of the 1992 Order). The change involved vehicle access tracks that were not for agriculture or forestry operations, and that will therefore from 1992 require planning permission from the local authority. However, new tracks are still being made without planning consent.

A chief concern of planning officers and others is that rules on permitted development are too lax. A little-noticed provision appeared in the 1992 Order, applying to Class 18 on agricultural buildings and operations, and also Class 22 on forestry buildings and operations. It stated that the formation or alteration of a private way was permitted only if the planning authority had been notified for a determination as to whether the authority's prior approval would be required. It stated further that the planning authority would have 28 days to determine whether prior approval was required. However, six months later under the GPDO Amendment Order No.(2), this provision was deleted by the Scottish Office. This deletion is revealing in indicating Scottish Office unwillingness to give planning authorities the ability to put even reasonable curbs on private landowners, even where this is clearly in the public interest, as here.

An important gap in the GPDO is that Class 8 allows for the formation, laying-out and construction of a means of access to a road which is not a trunk road or a classified road, where that access is required in connection with development permitted by any Class in this schedule (other than Class 7). Some have interpreted this as allowing a wide range of road development within a property. However, there is some uncertainty, for one experienced planner commented to me that he had always taken Class 8 as relating solely to the actual access to a road, and not to any road or track thereafter. My reading of the wording as stated above would confirm his interpretation. Nevertheless, clearly the regulations need review and clarification using unambiguous explicit wording.

Another gap is that Class 27 allows for the carrying out, on lands within the boundaries of a private road or private way, of works required for the maintenance or improvement of the road or way. Here, road or way is as defined under the Road Scotland Act 1984, where the definition is quite open and vague. Thus a big loophole is that 'maintenance' or 'improvement' to an existing track does not require planning consent, and yet can cause much damage. Indeed, on certain occasions and track sections the damage can exceed that caused by the original bulldozing or by careless construction of a brand new track, and can far exceed the environmental impact when a new track is given planning approval with useful conditions on excavation methods and reinstatement measures.

Hence there are various ways in which tracks have been constructed with either little or no oversight by planners. Such tracks have increased in recent years, under the provisions whereby other kinds of permitted development by statutory undertakers can take place, such as tracks to telecommunication sites.

Planning officers receive few applications currently for agricultural tracks. The main wave of such tracks has passed and agriculture is in a depressed state. However, there are still cases, as in decades back to the 1960s, where an owner claims that a track is agricultural when it is patently for sporting purposes. There are currently, again as in the past, cases where private landowners or forestry companies build tracks across the open hill, between a public road and a proposed area for tree planting or to an existing woodland, and contend that these do not need permission. There are a few cases where a statutory undertaker such as Forest Enterprise, a local authority, or the Crown uses its development rights inappropriately, but such cases are comparatively few.

Some track developers claim that they were unaware of the rules. This seems highly dubious, given that most of them are large landowners who retain lawyers and land agents with much expertise in knowing regulations concerning land, such as grant aid and taxation. Others, especially in remote areas, think they can get away with track construction without planning consent, due to lack of public concern or even lack of anyone from the public noticing new tracks; or to lack of political will in public agencies, or to ineffective enforcement powers. For local authorities and statutory bodies such as SNH, this includes the problems arising from implementing cumbersome procedures, as well as lack of staff and competing pressure from other work that may be regarded as of higher public importance.

Planning officers still receive a flow of problem cases, albeit not on the scale of 25 years ago. Also, despite recent notable cases in the central and west Highlands, it is still mainly an east-Highland issue, as in the 60s and more recent decades.

It should be noted that bringing all tracks into planning consent would not necessarily stop them being constructed, since the planning system starts from a presumption that development can take place. However, if the regulations were tightened, planners would be able to apply conditions to ensure that the location, standards of construction and finish were appropriate to the setting.

A more general problem is that planners are concerned mainly with development control of buildings, and relatively seldom have to deal with countryside issues such as forestry, flooding, and tracks. Their training has involved insufficient attention to issues of soils, hydrology, vegetation, excavation and reinstatement, and this applies also to staff in SNH and Historic Scotland. In consequence, the views of staff from SNH or HS after site visits have been superficial and inadequate, and planners have attached conditions which were cosmetic and unimportant, rather than fundamental for maximum reinstatement success. Hence planning officers and staff in SNH and HS could benefit from scientific information on the subject as well as estate owners and agents. One planner in the Highlands, considering an estate's preliminary suggestion in 2002 to bulldoze a vehicle track along the line of an existing narrow footpath, thought it would not need planning consent because it would involve mere upgrading of an existing track and hence would be permitted development.

To sum up, the proliferation of new poorly constructed hill tracks and of poor works during maintenance or upgrading of existing tracks has continued to date, in almost all cases without planning consent and hence without the useful conditions that could be attached to such consent. Also in almost all cases, works have been carried out with no attempt to fit the track into the landscape, with no measures to reduce bare ground or consequent run-off and soil erosion, and with no work on reinstatement. Clearly this is not in the wider public interest regionally or nationally. Many planning officers and others say there is an undeniable case for explicit tighter regulations and enforcement, which are decades overdue.

The General Permitted Development Order should be reviewed urgently, to bring new vehicle tracks and their upgrading under full planning control with effective enforcement. The GPDO also requires modernisation and removal of archaic anomalies and protectionism by bringing change of use in forestry and agriculture under planning control, including tracks or roads, and also felling and drainage operations. It is an obvious anomaly that a new track or road for agriculture or forestry is permitted development (next Chapter, paragraph 2), while a new track for shooting is not.

In 2005 the Scottish Executive went ahead with public consultation on proposals for a radical reform of the entire planning system in Scotland. This was an opportunity to change the regulations on tracks. On 24 December 2005 I sent a letter about these concerns to the Scottish Executive's Chief Planner Mr James G. Mackinnon, and reproduce it in the Appendix below. In short, my letter called for tighter control of hill tracks by improved regulations and in particular by zoning, for more consistent attitudes and decisions by the planning officers in local authorities, and for a greater understanding of the technical issues of soils, hydrology, vegetation and reinstatement among local authorities and Public Inquiry Reporters. In reply, Mr Mackinnon emphasised the review of the planning system, and observed that the issue of Permitted Development was part of this review. He also stated that over £2 million has been allocated in the next few years to support schemes to raise skills and knowledge in the planning profession.

A new Planning Bill was introduced in the Scottish Parliament in December 2005. One of the main aspects of this legislation was the formation of a National Planning Framework to set out new regulations for the use and development of land in Scotland. The new planning system was considered by the Parliament, and it was envisaged that eventually in 2008 the NPF will be issued. It has not yet been decided whether the NPF will be open to public inquiry, but obviously there are strong reasons for doing so, to increase accountability and democracy.

The above review was published in 2006 and recommended radical change in the Permitted Development Rights for agriculture and forestry, including vehicle tracks. Despite this, two successive governments have failed to act upon these recommendations, now with the current SNP Government (April 2011), after five years.

Chapter 8. Control of location, construction and reinstatement

This comprises two related aspects. One is better planning regulations for controlling the location and design of new tracks, including conditions involving procedures to minimise impact and maximise reinstatement. The second is technical expertise to inform planners, landowners, excavator operators and others involved with such control, so that the conditions attached to planning consent lead to maximal reinstatement success. This section deals with both.

All new vehicle hill tracks outside NSAs now require planning permission, except where they are for agriculture (Class 18(1)(b)), or for forestry under an approved Woodland Grant Scheme (Class 22(1)(b)).

Most local authorities do not have policies for hill tracks, but Aberdeenshire Council (AC) has plans that indicate refusal unless a proposed track would fit the landscape. AC's Local Plan Policies, Finalised Draft (30 April 2002), states, under Policy Env\23 on Vehicle Hill Tracks, 'Vehicle hill tracks, and extensions to them, will be refused unless they can be integrated satisfactorily into the landscape and minimise detrimental impact, such as soil erosion, on the environment including habitats and watercourses.'

'Justification. The aim of this policy is to protect upland areas from development of new or extended vehicle hill tracks, which could damage them, by designing new roads which follow existing contours and fit with existing landforms and landscape features. These upland areas include woodland and open moorland mostly over the 400m contour.'

'The bulldozing of tracks to be used for agricultural, forestry and particularly sporting purposes has led to scars across the hills, which are often visible across a very wide area and are prone to erosion. The continuation of such development is not in the best interests of the environment. Vehicle hill tracks must therefore be designed to fit into the landscape. They must not obliterate existing paths and historic trackways, and their design should minimise the need for engineering and road-related earthworks.'

In a case at Gleann an t-Slugain near Braemar (see Hill tracks in north-east Scotland since the 1980 regulations, 18., above), where Invercauld Estate carried out engineering operations with an excavator to widen and upgrade a former cart track, I did not inform Aberdeenshire Council until after four years had elapsed since the works, but I was then unaware that planning consent became necessary after 1997.

The Council's enforcement officer Mr Porter wrote in a letter of 31 January 2002 to me, 'The Town & Country Planning (Scotland) Act, 1997, Section 124, is specific in that it states that where there has been a breach of planning control consisting in the carrying out without planning permission of building, engineering, mining or other operation in, on, over or under land, no enforcement action may be taken after the end of the period of 4 years, beginning with the date on which the operation was substantially completed. The Planning Authority would therefore not be in a position to pursue a retrospective application in this case if development were proved to have occurred.'

It may be asked by the public whether this 4-year limit applies also to new buildings erected without planning approval. If not, there is a good case for the limit to be the same for tracks as for buildings.

With 'improvements' to private roads and ways (Class 27), the scope for damage is much greater, as developers at present can legitimately carry out works without planning consent, and such works can be obtrusive, causing side-effects such as run-off and erosion that can have impacts on others, including public roads and ditches. A proposal that all widening or other improvement should require planning permission might be viewed by some landowners as excessive, but it would be in the public interest, and has become necessary because most cases have involved severe damage and flouting of good track design by owners.

Also, it would be difficult to get explicit drafting if there were a compromise position, and this would inevitably lead to attempts by owners or their agents to circumvent the regulations by exploiting loopholes. Enforcement is difficult, especially on remote land where the work might not be reported until long after completion. An appropriate aid would be cross-compliance, where an owner forfeits the right to public grant or subsidies if he or she carries out a damaging action and refuses to comply with recommendations to bring the 'improvement' up to an acceptable standard.

Many expected that the formation of National Parks in Scotland would lead to far higher standards of control and construction. However, the Cairngorms National Park Authority showed no sign of this in its draft Interim Planning

Policy No. 3: Vehicle Hill-tracks, issued on 14 July 2004 for consultation. This document ignored normal planning practice on zoning, such as zoning industrial premises separately from residential areas. For example it made no attempt to zone sensitive areas that are outstanding for landscape or wildlife, by proposing a presumption against new tracks in such areas.. It included statements (p. 3) that 'It is in the very nature of sporting, agricultural and forest estates that vehicular access tracks will be required up hillsides' and 'If a new track is absolutely necessary, and there are no existing tracks that can be utilised, then it must be designed and built to fit-in, as far as possible, with the landscape.' The draft did not mention any assessment to check what is claimed by developers as 'absolutely necessary'.

Instead of emphasising control, most of the draft policy covered how to construct tracks. The sections on construction, including the diagrams, were technically incompetent. If followed, these detailed recommendations would have led to unnecessary extra problems with drainage, greater erosion, unsatisfactory driving surfaces, and poor reinstatement. This revealed inadequate knowledge among staff and Board members. The same technical flaws mar SNH's 2006 manual on constructed tracks (see SNH guide etc below, and Appendix).

It would benefit good practice if the Scottish Environment & Rural Affairs Department SERAD were to refuse grants or free advice for bulldozing a new track or road, or for its upgrading for agricultural or forestry purposes. Likewise, the FC should give no grants or free advice for the above for forestry purposes, if the routes lie partly or wholly outside land marked for an approved woodland grant scheme.

If an owner bulldozes a new track or road without planning consent, the planning authority should resolve that the track or road be removed, and the ground reinstated at the owner's expense to a standard determined by the authority. If the owner refuses, an enforcement order should be made and imposed, with realistic penalties.

When a planning application is made, the applicant should include detailed descriptions of procedures to ensure minimal environmental impact on landscape, vegetation, and soils including reduction of run-off and soil erosion, and maximal reinstatement success. If such described procedures are deemed insufficient, the planning approval should include conditions to ensure an acceptable outcome.

The production of a site survey should be essential, where an expert in soils, hydrology and vegetation walks the proposed route, noting vegetation and water features, digging occasional trial soil pits as checks, and tailoring the best route and the methods of excavation and drainage to suit the different soil types. This should include decisions on the optimal sites for culverts, with none on the most freely drained soils but several at close intervals such as every 10 m at wet flushes. If the track is intended for use by only light vehicles such as land rovers, there should be no need for any excavation or drainage on the most freely drained sandy or gravelly soils, and a marked route for wheel tracks to develop should be all that is necessary (for a good accessible example, see the wheel tracks on the moor south of Redburn, on Dinnet Estate south of Logie Coldstone.

Also essential should be the proviso that such an expert accompanies the excavator driver on the first part of the first day of work. The expert should also attend for a brief visit subsequently, if the track is more than 1 km long or if the soil types seen on the first day do not include those known to occur on the rest of the route.

Full comprehensive details of reinstatement are not given here, since technical information on the necessary procedures is available in publications and reports. Also, the main points are mentioned briefly in Technical Comments on the Etive Track (by A. Watson, in an Appendix below).

Watson & Bayfield (1988) made recommendations for improved reinstatement on an insensitively made road in Glen Ey. Bayfield (1988) gave a useful account on hill tracks generally, though it should be noted that the cut (uphill) bank in his cross-sectional diagram given by him is far too steep (>50°) for stability. Also, it is unwise to consider an uphill drain to catch overland run-off as standard. On freely drained soils without peat, such drains are unnecessary and can cause severe erosion, as occurred at the Lecht Ski Centre until they were in-filled. They are often excavated as a standard requirement in hill country with public tarmac roads, gravel roads, vehicle tracks, and footpaths constructed or repaired in recent decades. For example, the 'best practice guide' on repairs of upland footpaths in the UK (Davis & Loxham with Huggon 1996) states this without question, and illustrates it by photograph and drawing.

Another recent example was the consultation draft interim policy for vehicle hill-tracks by the Cairngorms National Park Authority in July 2004. This included the statement that 'ditches will be required on one or both sides....to keep water off the track. Obstructions in the base of the ditch (e.g. stones) will also cause erosion, ideally the water will be able to flow freely and slowly. The ditch should be at least 500 mm from the edge of the track, and approximately 500 mm wide and 300 mm deep, normally with a 'V'-shaped profile.' All of these recommendations, if implemented, would cause unnecessary impacts and would be likely to increase soil erosion.

Where soils are iron humus podzols or peaty podzols, cut-off drains up-slope usually burst the iron pan or other indurated layers that prevent erosion of the looser soil below the layer, and thereby can cause severe erosion including gullying. The potential problems created by disrupting a perched water-table also need to be considered in the field, and avoided by any excavation works for drains or for lowering the level of a track so as to ease the gradient for an ascent or descent.

A fairly detailed account of useful methods appeared in the 1996 environmental statement on proposed developments at Glencoe Ski Centre (Watson, Walker & Rae 1996), sent to and agreed by Highland Council, concerning a proposed car park and its banks, and drainage of them. The following quotations cover the salient points.

'For these banks, boulders should be deposited in decreasing size, next the parent material from which the soil has developed (the C horizon), then the B horizon material, followed by the A horizon material, and finally any organic matter (the H horizon). It is essential to utilise all available upper soil horizons below the turf, on top of the car park banks' (equally relevant to track banks). 'To prevent subsequent erosion, it is essential for the correct slope to be established on the banks, with an angle of not more than 30 degrees, and for the bare surfaces to be cloaked as the construction proceeds. The contractor should not regard this phase as a two-step construction, i.e. doing all the banking and only then proceeding with the covering. Moreover, banks should not be graded to form completely smooth surfaces, but should be left with an irregular configuration, as this looks more natural and helps reduce soil erosion....The excavated peat should be deposited as a veneer about 15 cm thick over the car park banks to provide a rooting medium for the final top dressing of turves, plant litter, seed etc....It is important to use a strict sequence for the stripping and stockpiling of turf and the underlying upper soil horizons, as an essential preparation for reinstatement of vegetation cover on fill slopes. Excavated turf and each of the upper soil horizons as described above should be stored separately on geotextile membrane, to maximize the success of reinstatement. Turves should be watered during storage, and storage should be brief, ideally no longer than two days. To reduce damage to soils and vegetation, excavators should not be used when ground is wet after recent heavy rain....Local turves should be used to re-vegetate any bare ground. Gaps between turves should be packed with topsoil or with peat. An excess of turf is virtually certain if stripping is carefully carried out. This turf could be used to re-vegetate the bare patches nearby.' Turf and turves in the above quotations involve surface vegetation, along with the main set of plant roots and plant litter, and also the uppermost soil horizons that contain them.

An important, often overlooked aspect of reinstatement (see Watson *et al.* 1996), is that excavation should not be completed before reinstatement works begin. To ensure minimal impact and maximal reinstatement, excavation and reinstatement should both be done each day, excavating the first section and then doing reinstatement works on it that day, before moving on to the next section (see also Appendix below).

From 50 years experience of new vehicle hill tracks, it is possible to make tentative conclusions on the pace of recovery of bare ground and future prospects of recovery. The accounts for each individual track refer to this problem, but an overall assessment may be of some value. This cannot be wholly objective or quantitative, because so little formal quantitative monitoring of recovery has been done.

If vegetation, topsoil or peat, and upper horizons of subsoil are saved carefully and put back in reverse order on the same day, then reinstatement of track spoil can be almost complete that day and wholly complete within one growing season. If they are not saved and reinstated properly, and are buried under infertile subsoil at a depth too great for plants to survive, then recovery of spoil is bound to be very slow. Recovery rates on spoil are fastest in sheltered locations at low altitude, and slowest in exposed places at high altitude where plant cover is sparse and soils are infertile. Exposed sites at high altitude recover at a faster rate if the soil has been derived from base-rich parent materials, such as limestone or diorite, than if derived from acidic hard granite or quartzite. Heath-dominated vegetation on spoil heaps suffers more damage and recovers more slowly than grass-dominated vegetation, other factors being equal.

Because low gradients are associated with less run-off and soil erosion than steep gradients, vegetation recovery on track surfaces and especially in the middle of the track surface is faster on low gradients than on steep ones. Likewise, if excavated banks are deposited at an angle greater than that of stability (around 30°), especially if the top of the bank is left overhanging, recovery will be extremely slow because of continual movement of the bank surface. Again, if the parent material is acidic hard rock, or the subsoil has been derived from very freely draining infertile fluvio-glacial deposits from such rock, recovery will be far slower than if the deposits are in moraines or till from acidic rock, and slower still than if they are are derived from base-rich rock. If the main underlying soil is peat greater than 0.5 m thickness, then recovery of banks will be very slow unless they are at a low angle.

If a proposed track cannot be aligned wholly to avoid thick peat or other very wet sites, then the best solution is to deposit gravel for the track on to the ground surface, rather than attempting to excavate down to subsoil. This has been successfully done on roads to wind-farm sites on land with peat several metres thick, e.g. at Novar in Ross & Cromarty, and Beinn Ghlas near Oban (see below, Some examples of good practice).

If vegetation is heath-dominated, reinstatement is most successful if excavation and reinstatement procedures are carried out during the plants' dormant season, because evapo-transpiration losses from excavated heath are so high during the growing season that much of the green foliage dies and even whole plants may die. For this reason, works with heath should ideally be carried out in late September–early October. One should avoid the main period of frost, cold winds and snow later in winter and in early spring, when freeze-thaw actions and even simply low air temperatures, especially when accompanied by low humidity, can severely damage or kill green foliage by rapid evapo-transpiration leading to winter browning.

Grass-dominated swards are best excavated and reinstated as early in the growing season as possible, allowing the greatest time for subsequent growth recovery later in the same growing season. Irrespective of anything stated above, works should not be done during heavy rain or within a few days of it, because of the increased damage to soil and vegetation by excavators used in soft wet ground.

It is possible for an experienced operator, with appropriate technical guidance from someone with expertise in geomorphology, soils, hydrology and vegetation, to take a route which avoids many difficulties and produces an eventual result with rapid recovery and good reinstatement, where even the track surface becomes covered with vegetation (for examples, see Appendix). At the other extreme, the worst examples of cheap bulldozed tracks on steep gradients, inadequate parent materials, and high altitudes have recovered so slowly that most spoil heaps, banks and track surfaces are still largely bare after 35 years. In many cases this will continue until banks are re-aligned at a lower gradient and until reseeding or placing of native turf is used and/or addition of humus in the form of a thin layer of peat.

The most important objective for achieving good standards is to increase awareness, including not only the general public, local and national politicians, and officers in local and national authorities, but also estate owners and staffs, farmers, land agents, forestry consultants and moorland consultants. A secondary but important objective is to dissuade private estates and other organisations and individuals from building needless tracks and, where they feel they can justify them, to go through the proper procedures, having availed themselves of appropriate technical advice aimed at minimising environmental impact and maximising reinstatement success.

Chapter 9. Some examples of good practice

Priestlaw Moor, Berwickshire

One example is a road across this moor, illustrated in a photograph accompanying an article by Bayfield (1988). When planning Torness power station, the South of Scotland Electricity Board required new pylons across the Lammermuirs and a road giving access to a lorry up to a 40 t specification. Landowner Peter D. Straker-Smith insisted that the hill vegetation and top 15 cm of soil with its seed bank be excavated carefully, put aside, and replaced. Alex McLarty of Crieff carried out the work in 1987, leaving the spoil in a long low line on either side of the road and covering it wholly with the excavated turves, beside a road with a surface of packed gravel. The operator buried all boulders under subsoil or peat, and left no bare subsoil above the surface. The result even immediately afterwards was fairly satisfactory.

I have two comments. One is that where tall heather (late building, mature and degenerate phases) was excavated, some of this had died or was dying, as shown in photographs. To reduce this with future tracks, each excavated turf of tall heather should occupy a larger area and involve a greater soil depth (e.g. 60 x 60 cm in area and 40 cm deep). The second comment is that the B horizon of subsoil, which contains a valuable source of nutrients, albeit less than the A horizon or topsoil, was not part of the specification. Ideally this should be removed after the removal of topsoil and vegetation, stored separately, and put back in reverse order.

Wind farm at Novar, Ross & Cromarty

National Wind Power Ltd constructed new roads on moorland at Novar Estate in east Ross-shire in 1996–97 to allow heavy machines to reach turbine sites. Environmental consultant Dr Tom Dargie and National Wind Power Ltd planned the routes so that roads would be mostly hidden from surrounding glens and public roads. Contractor Edward Mackay of Brora constructed the roads to a high standard. On areas of thick peat, gravel was laid on a geotextile layer on the vegetation surface. All reinstatement involved excavated turf, not reseeding. National Wind Power Ltd subsequently used the same contractor and similar methods at a wind farm on moorland at Beinn Ghlas near Oban.

At Novar in June 1998 I noted (Watson 1998) several points that would have led to less impact and better reinstatement had they been in the contract. Referring to banks, I stated that 'it would have been better not to create such a smooth even surface, which looks unnatural. A rougher surface would look more natural, help plant colonisation, reduce erosion, and be cheaper to produce....Heather turves were excavated with inadequate thickness of soil, and the result was that many had died....Heather turves should be at least 6 inches thick, and preferably thicker. Gaps between and around heather turves had exacerbated these problems....it would be useful to pack such gaps with peat or mineral soil...The timing of storage and reinstatement should be considered carefully, emphasising reinstatement as soon after as possible, preferably within a day or two.'

In summary, the main flaws were a) heather excavated with turves too small in area and with inadequate thickness of topsoil, resulting in much death of plants, b) bog vegetation laid on some steep freely drained gravel banks, leading to plant death, c) no separate excavation, storage, and re-use in reverse order of turf, topsoil, and upper subsoil (B) horizons, and d) no reinstatement within a day or two of the excavation, section by section. These were not criticisms of the contractor but of the technical specifications given to him. In discussions on site with me, he was aware of the importance of items a)–d).

This raises the more general issue that a number of contractors can do a very good job, if the technical specifications are adequate and someone with experience of the inter-relationships of hill soils, hydrology, vegetation and reinstatement discusses issues on site with the contractor.

Glen Feshie, Inverness-shire

This case involves works funded by a later landowner so as to reduce the lasting impact from crude construction by earlier owners. A start was made in 2001 to re-profile some tracks that had been constructed in the 1960s. The kennels track was re-constructed by reducing the gradient of the batter on the upper side, removing and separating turf, and elevating and double cambering the road surface. Removed turf was then laid on exposed gravel on the banks. This greatly reduced the visual impact and the erosion of the track surface. Contractor Alex McLarty of Crieff did the work, but it stopped following the financial demise of estate owner Mr Helmersen.

However, since 2001 a Danish estate-owner Mr Flemming Skouboe has carried out similar works on tracks made in the 60s and 70s. This involved use of an excavator by McLarty to re-profile the originally steep cut and fill banks, so as to reduce visual scars and create a smoother running surface for vehicles. The operator raised the camber to reduce run-off and erosion, and moved vegetation to reduce the amount of bare ground. As a result, the width of bare ground declined from 10 m to as little as 2.5 m. The edges of the track camber were re-seeded with a mixture of heather and wavy hair grass. This work included the track west of Slochd Mor. A hill walker reported that an excavator in September 2002 was greatly widening the track on Carn Dearg Mor, but it seems likely that this was a temporary phase leading to less impact as on the other old tracks that have been tackled.

Scottish Natural Heritage, Invereshie, Inverness-shire

At their holding in the Cairngorms NNR, the Nature Conservancy in 1967 upgraded tracks that had been bulldozed for timber extraction in 1940–45. This proved a classic example of how not to construct a hill track. The worst section involved a 150 m loop at 869010, where track gradients exceeded 18°. Surface run-off later caused some scouring and erosion. Further west, along the original extraction route at 866012, the track became completely washed out in the 1970s, due to inadequate drains. SNH eventually installed effective drains in 1993, and these have worked well.

Removal of tracks on Mar Lodge Estate, Aberdeenshire

Since purchasing this estate, the National Trust for Scotland has emphasised landscape and wildlife including the concept of wild land. As part of this policy, the Trust has removed several tracks that were bulldozed into remote parts of the estate several decades before. The tracks were narrowed down to footpath width, along with reinstatement work on either side. The landscape impact of the treated tracks has been greatly reduced, as well as soil erosion. These results are a recent demonstration that restoration work has been successful even at high altitudes on infertile soils. This rejects the frequently stated but erroneous assertion that restoration work does as much damage as the original construction and so should not be attempted. The Appendices below give details.

Removal of track on Balmoral Estate, Aberdeenshire

In 2006, 'A one-kilometre section of eroded hill-track was re-vegetated back to heather moorland. This was accomplished by transplanting heather turfs and re-seeding with locally harvested heather seed and a native grass seed mix' (Balmoral Estate website). It was a bulldozed vehicle track on Broad Cairn above Allan's Hut.

Well made Victorian track by pick and shovel, Glen Beg, Balmoral Estate, 27 September 1954.

Well made track by Dalnaspidal Estate in 2009 on wet heath, 9 August 2009.

Bibliography

Aitken, R. (1995). Vehicle tracks in Scotland's hills: a background note. Report from the Footpath Management Project to SNH, Edinburgh.

Baldwin, J.R. (1987). A better future for SSSIs? Scottish Wildlife, New Series 3, 5.

Bayfield, N. (1988). Hill roads - for better or for worse. Joseph Nickerson Reconciliation Project Annual Report 4, 28–29.

Brown, C. (2010). Act now to stop the spread of hill tracks. Scottish Wild Land News 75, 4–7.

Campbell, C. (2003). Bell tolls for historic road. Leopard Magazine 297, 12–13.

Carus, H. (2011). Hill tracks campaign update. Scottish Mountaineer 50, 65.

Cook, J.A. (2003a). Invercauld hill tracks quandary. Mountain Views 51, 14–15.

Cook, J.A. (2003b). Controversy at Corgarff. Mountain Views 52, 14-15.

Cook, J.A. (2006). Keeping tracks. Mountain Views 57, 3–6.

Countryside Commission for Scotland (1978). Vehicular tracks in upland Scotland. CCS, Battleby, Perth.

Countryside Commission for Scotland (1987). Environmental design and management of ski areas in Scotland: A practical handbook. CCS, Battleby, Perth.

Countryside Commission for Scotland (1988). 20th Annual Report. Battleby, Perth.

Dales, M. (2002). Stopping tracks in wild places. The Scottish Mountaineer 14, 37.

Davis, P. & Loxham, J. with Huggon, G. (1996). Repairing upland path erosion. A best practice guide. Countryside Commission & British Upland Footpath Trust.

Edwards, R. (1996). Queen evades wildlife laws. New Scientist 2015, 4.

Gauld, J.H., Bell, J.S., Towers, W. & Miller, D.R. (1991). The measurement and analysis of land cover changes in the Cairngorms. Macaulay Land Use Research Institute, Aberdeen.

Johnston, H. (2006). Hope for control of upland tracks. Scottish Wild Land News 67, 7–8.

McNeish, C. (2010). Hill problem looks to have been side-tracked. Badenoch & Strathspey Herald, 9 February.

Maison, J. (1999). Glen Doll. Mountain Views 44, 23–24.

Newbury, M. (2006). SNH hill tracks manual. An MC of S view. The Scottish Mountaineer 32, 42.

Peacock, P. (2010). Peter Peacock MSP writes. Mountain Views 62, 8–9.

Scottish Development Department (1980). Development control in National Scenic Areas. SDD Circular No. 20. Edinburgh.

Scottish Natural Heritage (2006). Constructed tracks in the Scottish uplands. A 'good practice guide' by Land Use Consultants with assistance of A.D. Cruden Associates & Professor P. Bishop of University of Glasgow. SNH, Battleby, Perth.

Thompson, P.S. & Thompson, D.B.A. (1991). Greenshanks Tringa nebularia and long-term studies of breeding waders. Ibis 133, Supplement 1, 99–112.

Tyldesley, D. & Associates (1996). The Cairngorms Partnership legislative, policy and planning framework. The Cairngorms Partnership, Grantown on Spey.

Watson, A. (1984). A survey of vehicular hill tracks in North-east Scotland for land use planning. Journal of Environmental Management 18, 345–353.

Watson, A. (1998). Some comments on the Novar site visit and potential relevance to construction and reinstatement works ar Beinn Ghlas. Report to National Wind Power Ltd.

Watson, A. & Bayfield, N.G. (1988). Ground reinstatement on the Glen Ey road. Institute of Terrestrial Ecology, Banchory.

Watson, A. & North East Mountain Trust (2010). A survey of vehicular hill tracks in North East Scotland, 1981–82. Published and distributed by NEMT, Aberdeen.

Watson, A., Walker, A.D. & Rae, S. (1996). Environmental statement on proposed developments at Glencoe Ski Centre and environmental aspects of the 1996 Management Plan. 49 pp.

Wightman, A. (1996). Who owns Scotland? Canongate, Edinburgh.

Appendices

A. Report on all-terrain vehicle track above Loch Etive

By Mike Newbury

Following enquiries from the media and representations to the Mountaineering Council of Scotland, this track was inspected (for the first 2km or so from the south) on 20 April 1998 by Mike Dales (Access & Conservation Officer, MC of S) and Mike Newbury (Member of MC of S Access and Conservation Committee and the then Chairman of the British Upland Footpath Trust), in company with Andrew Campbell (Area Officer, SNH), Richard Leishman (Area Officer, SNH) and Bill Green (Forest Officer). Mike Newbury re-inspected the track from end to end on 29 June 2000, with Dougal Roy of the MCofS Access and Conservation Committee.

The track, 2.5 m wide, starts at the end of the forest road at Ordnance Survey grid reference 081405 (opposite Inverghuisachan Point), runs northeastward generally about 200 m from the shoreline, for 5 km, stopping abruptly in a bog at a point about 150 m above the shore path, some 300 m from the end of the public road near the head of Loch Etive. The track was built in the winter of 1997–98 by a local contractor, Willie Buchanan. We gathered that he had no previous experience of this kind of work. The cost was at the very low rate of about £2 per metre. We did not learn of any detailed written specification.

The reason given for the construction of the track was to provide an 'ATV bike route' to facilitate work on the regeneration of the semi-natural woodlands in this area, parts of which comprise an SSSI (Ard Trilleachan) and all within a National Scenic Area. There are extensive oak woods formerly coppiced for tannin bark and charcoal (with ancient hearths visible) merging into relict pine woods, with moribund holly, and extensive birch regeneration particularly where the ground was deep ploughed some years ago. We were told that it is intended to encourage a mosaic structure with open glades which also form important habitats.

We were told that a fence surrounds the whole area of some 600 ha, and that this fence was being renewed, but that exclosures of about 1ha were also necessary. For the purposes of constructing and maintaining the exclosures, culling and extracting deer (to be reduced in density from 14 to about 8 per 100-ha) and management generally, it was said to be necessary to take access by quad bike (rather than by boat), and hence the new track.

On re-inspection we found signs of use by bicycles but no recent signs of vehicular use, and there were trees lying across the track, having apparently lain there for many months. The occasional tufts of tall rushes and tall grasses which are growing on the track surface without signs of breaking or bruising confirmed the absence of vehicles. We found that deer-fencing exclosures of varying sizes had been constructed, and a continuous fence along the contour some 200–300m in horizontal distance above the track.

There is a right of way footpath running separately along the shore. This is wet and bouldery near the head of the Loch, but where the track approaches it in the woodland it appeared pleasant and good underfoot, and walkers who have used it confirm that this applies most of the way. Nevertheless, the Scottish Rights of Way Society, whose sign at the road end says 'Public footpath to Bonawe', have a way-mark pointing away from the path in a direction up through the bog to the end of the new track, and thence along it. The new track appears to be used as a 'challenge' route by mountain bikers, but use by walkers seems light. I was told that few would prefer 'this undulating monstrosity' to the attractive loch-side right of way.

A photographic record was taken on both occasions. The general width of the running surface is about 2.5 m, but the overall width of disturbed ground extends over some 7.5 m, forming a strip which I was told is visible from Ben Cruachan. It will be obvious from Ben Starav (except for the more heavily wooded sections when the trees are in full leaf), and of course it dominates the near view of the walker or cyclist using the track.

The upside cut sections of the route had been scooped out unevenly and left raw, with no attempt to salvage and re-lay vegetation, or the thin horizons of topsoil and upper subsoil, and indeed much of these materials is buried beneath infertile lower subsoil horizons. Despite the generally low cross gradients, the contractor had produced some high over-steepened undercut banks, which looked just as raw on the later inspection as when newly dug. Some trees (in particular some good oaks) have been left with roots exposed.

The upside ditch comprises a series of deep irregular troughs. The cross-drain pipes are set too high, so as to be useless except for flood-water, but natural drainage is apparently good as the troughs were dry except for a few pools well below the pipe inlets (although re-inspection was in unusually dry weather). There has been no attempt to conceal the projecting pipe-ends with reclaimed stone and turves, and this could not be done in any case because of the inappropriate pipe levels; indeed, some of the pipes are liable to become exposed on the surface after further scouring.

The track surface is in places lumpy and irregularly cambered; and because it is of granite-derived subsoil, I considered it liable to scour, particularly as some of the track undulations reach a measured gradient of 20 degrees. However, re-inspection revealed little scour, possibly because of very light use and little water running on to it; also perhaps, the clay content. Occasional patches of vegetation have colonised the track surface and the up-slope ditch. The track in the woodland sections is generally stonier, in places bouldery, with sometimes good re-colonisation of vegetation.

The downside fill slopes generally comprise loose spillage of subsoil, stones and turves, along with granite boulders which had been left wherever they happened to roll. These slopes showed generally good re-vegetation on re-inspection. Uprooted trees had been left lying. No attempt had been made to mould the slope or press down irregularities. The loose boulders were less evident among the re-vegetation on re-inspection, but looked stark without the mosses and lichens so abundant on the naturally-occurring boulders.

There were ancient industries here, which finally ceased about 1870 with the closure of the Bonawe Iron Smelter, and the evidence is now barely perceptible, but in present circumstances, the impact of heavy powered machinery should have been minimised at the outset.

The route is unpleasant underfoot for the walker, with a hard, gritty, sometimes stony and even bouldery surface; and although the track winds in places, its embanked form of construction continues over the folds of ground, producing a tiresome series of steep switchbacks. I was assured of future maintenance as required, but no maintenance or ameliorative works are apparent.

Conclusions

SNH and FE are to be acclaimed for setting about the regeneration of these native woodlands, which appeared to have been too long suppressed by too many deer. However, the track represents a serious intrusion into 'wild land'* and in execution, its construction is poor by any standards. It is unsightly on both near and distant views in an area where particular sensitivity is required in terms of landscape, and without significant further work, natural healing is likely to take many years and ultimately to remain incomplete. Moreover, by the re-routing of walkers, the ancient footpath along the shore, which follows a better and more interesting line, is likely to become overgrown and lost. We consider (on advice) that there is no overriding need for the track, and that it should be obliterated and the ground restored.

**Notes*

(1) 'Wild land' is defined in The Scottish Office National Planning Policy Guideline (NPPG 14) of January 1999 as 'uninhabited and often relatively inaccessible countryside where the influence of human activity on the character and quality of the environment has been minimal'. Moreover, in paragraph 16 'The most sensitive landscapes may have little or no capacity to accept new development. Some of Scotland's remoter mountain and coastal areas possess an elemental quality from which many people derive psychological and spiritual benefits. Such areas are very sensitive to any form of development or intrusive human activity and planning authorities should take great care to safeguard their wild land character.'

(2) The Town and Country Planning (Restriction of Permitted Development) (National Scenic Areas) (Scotland) Direction 1987 requires that a formal application for planning permission should be made to the Planning Authority for vehicular tracks in National Scenic Areas, and if the Authority is minded to grant permission they should formally consult SNH in terms of the Town and Country Planning (Notification of Applications) (National Scenic Areas) (Scotland) Direction 1987; and if they approved, SNH should advise in writing and the Authority should then issue planning consent with appropriate conditions. (The wording of the Directions refers to the Countryside Commission for Scotland which has since been subsumed with the Nature Conservancy Council for Scotland into Scottish Natural

Wooden slats up steep slope to grouse-butts opposite Edinglassie Lodge, Strathdon, owned by Lord Cowdray, effective for vehicles, prevention of erosion, and landscape, June 1984.

Heritage. The consultation should therefore be conducted with reference to the duties of SNH in CCS role, not as NCCS, under which consent was given to operations in the SSSI under the Wildlife and Countryside Act.)

The Scottish Development Department Circular/1980, paragraph 3, asks Planning Authorities 'to pay particular attention to all applications for development in National Scenic Areas, as regards the grant or refusal of Planning Permission and the conditions attached to it' and refers to these areas as 'by definition a national resource'. We took this up with the Planning Authorities concerned, namely Argyll & Bute Council and Highland Council as regards their respective sections of the track, requesting that they enforce removal. It appears there had been some informal contact with the former, within whose area the track started, but that Highland Council was unaware of it.

It emerged that Forest Enterprise may well have Crown status covering the operation, requiring a 'Notice of Proposed Development' to the Planning Authority instead of an Application for Planning Permission. The procedure, which is roughly parallel, follows Scottish Development Circular No. 21/1984 (as amended).

No progress was made with Argyll & Bute Council, but on 7 March 2000, the Head of Development & Building Control of Highland Council wrote:- 'I remain of the consideration that the track requires permission through a 'Notice of Proposed Development'. Given the background to the case I have asked for comment from Forest Enterprise as well as from Argyll & Bute Council and Scottish Natural Heritage. Subject to their advice, I will then seek an application from Forest Enterprise.;

Subsequently, a retrospective Notice of Proposed Development was submitted to both Councils, and MC of S have responded, seeking restoration of the ground.

(Notwithstanding representations in this case, Forest Enterprise, with SNH sanction, made a similar track to the Corrie of Fee in Angus, also in a National Scenic Area. For many years, trampling on shaded vegetation on poorly drained soils along a restricted route through a dense conifer plantation had produced localised quagmires. The constructed track took a more freely drained route and is walkable. However, it incorporates tree stumps, loose brashings from cut branches, and unsorted stones which increasingly come to the surface due to freeze-thaw action. Following representations from MCofS and others, a retrospective Notice of Proposed Development was submitted in that case to Angus Council. A specification was drawn up by Martin McCrorie, an experienced upland path consultant, for converting the track to a properly constructed and landscaped footpath to the Corrie of Fee. We await seeing this specification put into effect.)

Issues arising

1. Given that Ard Trilleachan at Loch Etive is part SSSI and all NSA, and of 'wild land' quality, a presumption against disturbance (particularly disturbance by motor vehicles) might be expected. Instead, there has been penetration of the last remaining undisturbed area, northwards from the end of the road built in the 1960s and 70s for abortive forestry plantations.

We questioned whether there was an overriding need for this track. On 8 January, 1999, SNH's then-Chairman, Magnus Magnusson wrote, 'There are good reasons for the track to exist and these are detailed below. However, we do agree with you that, in retrospect, we did not adequately consider the impact of the work on the amenity and landscape of an area designated as an NSA. We regret this.' (The main reasons given by Mr. Magnusson were as follows: 'For some time we have been encouraging Forest Enterprise to undertake more active management of the native woodlands of Ard Trilleachan in order to secure their regeneration and expansion. In our view it is now pursuing a very welcome scheme to ensure the long term survival of this very valuable wood....Forest Enterprise is engaged in safeguarding the woodland by erecting a boundary fence, by erecting enclosures both within and outwith the boundary fence, and by controlling deer. The ATV track will be used by staff and contractors engaged in these activities, both now and during the period when maintenance of these structures and continuing deer control is required. The management plan envisages a reduction in deer numbers to around 8 per 100 ha. At this level, natural regeneration is still likely to be restrained by grazing pressure -hence the additional exclosures....SNH consented to the provision of a track because it seemed that the balance of advantage lay in not hindering FE in carrying out deer management work...').

We referred the SNH explanation to Dr. Adam Watson and Dick Balharry, who have had long expertise on deer research, natural tree regeneration, practical deer culling and reduction of deer densities to increase natural regeneration.

Independently they were, and remain, of the opinion that the track, boundary fence and exclosure fences were not necessary to achieve deer reductions sufficient to allow a net gain in tree regeneration. In particular, they saw no reason for the assumption that deer densities should be reduced only down to 8 deer per ha.

I have recently noted an FE sign near Glenmore Lodge, headed 'DEER FENCE REMOVAL'. It refers to capercaillie and blackgame mortality from deer fences (one of a several objections) and says 'Forest Enterprise (with financial assistance from the European Agriculture Guidance and Guarantee Fund) have removed approximately 21.5 km of deer fencing in 1998–99 from their forests in Strathspey....It is hoped that by controlling the population of deer through culling, the need for fencing will diminish'. People may well ask why FE is erecting deer fences at Loch Etive when it is concerned about the need to remove them at Glen More.

Apart from the Ard Trilleachan exclosures (which distort the mosaic of natural regeneration), the continuous fence running roughly parallel with the track is of particular concern. It prevents the natural movement of the remaining deer up and down the hill. By excluding the middle and upper slopes, into which fragments of the existing woodland extend, it excludes naturally regenerating tree seedlings in these areas from protection. This barrier is likely to lead to heavier use by deer in these areas, with consequently greater impacts than before the fence was erected. Especially important is the potential for very rare scrub and other plant communities around what should be the natural tree line. That is, unless there is to be adequate fencing higher up near the watershed, but this would be very intrusive in the open hill landscape and obstructive to both deer and hill-walkers, and would render the new lower fence redundant.

<u>2</u>. Since the FE and SNH officers concerned insisted that this is an ATV track and not a footpath, and since it is within an NSA, a Notice of Proposed Development should have been submitted to the local authority and publicised, to allow public consultation. It would then have been considered by the local authority's planning officers in a report to the Council, who could have raised objections to the development, or approved with recommendations on the standards of construction. Only after persistent representations from MCofS, is this process now taking place.

<u>3</u>. We asked whether SNH have a policy on the management and restoration of bulldozed tracks. I understood that less than 10 years previously, there was considerable controversy over an ATV track at the head of Glen Feshie, although it was shorter, less conspicuous and better constructed than the Loch Etive track.

At the same time as the Loch Etive track was being gouged out by FE, NTS were embarking upon the removal of bulldozed tracks on their Mar Lodge Estate, with SNH assistance. NTS had decided that the vehicular tracks were unnecessary for the increased deer culling that NTS wished to pursue in order to achieve natural tree regeneration without fencing. Since the tracks had become established pedestrian routes, NTS decided to reduce the wide tracks to narrow footpaths and reinstate any remaining disturbed ground.

It seemed invidious that SNH were simultaneously a party to the formation of a new bulldozed track in another special area of the Highlands, a track said to be necessary for achieving the same aim as the NTS. If, as we are advised, reductions in deer density and increases in tree regeneration at Ard Trilleachan could be achieved without a track, there is a strong case for the Ard Trilleachan track to be removed and the ground re-instated. Since the Ard Trilleachan track did not follow an established pedestrian route as at Mar Lodge, it should be removed completely, and not reduced to a footpath.

<u>4</u>. Given that the construction of a track was seen by FE and SNH as imperative, we asked whether SNH have standards appropriate for this special 'wild land' location bearing in mind the NSA designation. It would seem that the standards applied by SNH to upland path construction are appropriate here also. If one accepts that non-indigenous materials must be used, should not the cross-drain pipes be permanently buried and their projecting ends concealed by stonework, turf etc.? Should not the side slopes be landscaped and the verges turfed? This has been achieved with machine construction in many other locations, including the Storr Path in former Forestry Commission woodland near Portree, the new footpath/stalkers pony path through the plantation at Kernsary near Poolewe, and parts of the West Highland Way. All were part funded by SNH. When I demonstrated the normal practice for such high-quality pathworks using illustrations from the BUFT Upland Path Award Report 1997, the FE and SNH officers concerned seemed to consider this approach to construction work inapplicable or even bizarre.

It would seem that guidelines have been under consideration by SNH, because a report to SNH on the use of machinery in path-making is in circulation among path managers.

We asked whether SNH were now able to define and monitor standards, in particular in sensitive locations, and whether they would ensure that an appropriate standard is specified, monitored and enforced for any vehicular tracks which they are required to sanction in future.

In any case, hand finishing should have been employed in this sensitive location on the lines already indicated above, and now detailed in the practical advice contained in 'Upland Pathwork: Construction Standards for Scotland' available from SNH. This includes the laying of recovered turf on side slopes and verges, and the correct building of stonework over the ends of piped culverts.

5. It was to be assumed that FE/FC and SNH have landscape advisers. The cutting of a highly visible scar through a National Scenic Area would seem to demand specialist advice, but it did appear to us on site that it was not asked for or not taken.

6. We did not seek to blame the local officers concerned, as they appeared to have no instruction or training in landscape matters, although some sensitivity might have been expected and they might have been more wary of a relatively inexperienced contractor offering a cheap job. We asked that FE and SNH should examine their delegation of responsibilities and ensure that where local officers are responsible for such work, they are given appropriate technical advice and support, particularly where a specialist in one field has responsibility in a different field. I asked to be assured that procedures are in place to prevent a repetition of the Loch Etive problem elsewhere (but see the note on Corrie of Fee, above).

7. After our first inspection, the Forest District Manager sent a letter to me stating: 'There remains further finishing work to be done on the new track which may improve the appearance and the evenness of the surface pavement. Periodic maintenance will be carried out to effect any necessary repairs to the running surface and the track drainage. I confirm also that we are willing to monitor the recovery of the track-line and should there be insufficient natural healing and re-vegetation within two to three years, then we can certainly consider whether any further remedial work may be appropriate.'

This appeared inadequate in view of the poor construction described above and portrayed in photographs. As at June 2000, little or no natural re-vegetation had taken place, except on the down slopes, short woodland sections of track, and parts of the upper ditch; nor was any ameliorative work evident.

8. The question arose at the time of first inspection of whether the new track should be continued through to the public road near the head of Loch Etive. I asked to be assured of prior public consultation, to include responsible bodies such as MCofS, before any action was taken. Only a protective road-less gap of less than ½ km remains.

9. This track, if it were to remain, would likely be used by the public in place of the present less obvious shore path - indeed, it was newly way-marked at the time of later inspection. Since the shore path is and remains the right of way, the two local authorities have statutory powers to maintain it. Were they to adopt the line of the new track instead, it would present maintenance problems with its many 15–20 degree undulations (given significant use by walkers and cyclists) if local authorities ever come to be in a position to take path maintenance seriously. Furthermore, the new track follows a tedious line (see above) without the shore vistas of the old path, and would therefore be a wholly inadequate substitute.

Mike Newbury, July 2000 (MA in Estate Management (Cantab), FRICS, Member of the Access & Conservation Committee of the Mountaineering Council of Scotland and of the British Upland Footpath Trust's Executive Committee)

Technical comments by Adam Watson on Etive track, from photographs

When much of the disturbed ground is to end as a gravel vehicle track with no turf, as here, far more turf is available at the start than that needed to reinstate non-track bare surfaces later. So, if excavation is only moderately careful, there should be enough turf to cloak all bared verges and banks. The photographs show that the operator had excavated many turves, which he laid in concentrated patches on downside fill slopes. However, in the end most of the fill slopes had no turf, and all the cut slopes had none, so wastage must have been very large. Most turf must have become unavailable by being buried under boulders and subsoil.

It is manifest that most topsoil or peat was not excavated and stored for later reinstatement, and likewise the upper (more fertile) horizons of subsoil (B1 and B2 horizons). As in the case of turves (above), most of the fertile soil material must have been rendered unavailable through burial under boulders and subsoil. Some topsoil or peat was laid in patches on fill slopes and verges, but most of these were left with infertile subsoil (B3 and C horizons, and rocks) on the surface. Also, it is evident on the photographs that most of the topsoil or peat had overlain glacial till with a high content of clay, and that much of the exposed subsoil on cut banks and also much of the deposited subsoil on fill banks and verges comprised till. Such till with a content of clay is poor for vegetation colonisation if the till is left on the surface. It should have received a thin cloaking of topsoil or of peat to a thickness ideally of about 5 cm, but with anything from 1 to 8 cm being greatly preferable to leaving the clay surface bare.

Cut banks should have been no more than 30°, and smoothed, though with small undulations to mimic a natural appearance, minimise erosion and aid plants to colonise. No overhanging turf or soil should have been left at the top of cut banks.

Large boulders that were partly above ground level and hence supporting rock lichens should have been deposited lichen side upwards. Large boulders from below ground level should have been piled in stable angular fashion at the bottom of downside areas intended to become fill slopes and verges, with small boulders above them and subsoil only above that. If there were too many big boulders for this treatment throughout, hollows should have been selected, vegetation, topsoil and upper subsoil horizons excavated carefully and stockpiled separately, and then each hollow should have been filled with large boulders. This should have been followed by smaller boulders, and then cobbles, subsoil, topsoil and vegetation in the appropriate reverse sequence, if necessary forming a mound where previously there was a hollow.

Many operators can work to high standards, if shown by someone competent in soils and reinstatement, and with understanding of landforms, hydrology and vegetation. Such a person should tell the operator the aim of the work, why these procedures are recommended for this special site, and how this will produce a show-piece resulting in praise and good publicity for the operator. Such a technical adviser should explore the least damaging route beforehand by a site inspection, helped by soil pits and probes to measure peat thickness, noting also geomorphological and hydrological features and their relationships with soils, vegetation, and likely reinstatement success. None of this occurred at Loch Etive. In my view, no track was needed, given the stated objectives for the site. However, even if one assumes for the sake of argument that a track was necessary, it is surprising that such inadequate preparations were made before the contractor was hired.

B. Site inspection of Rinraoich track, Rothiemurchus, October 1998

Introduction

Following preliminary inspection of this track and others involved in recent publicity, I made a more detailed inspection on 15 October 1998, accompanied by Dr Stuart Rae. We counted cut trees and took colour photographs. The following notes refer to the track from a ford over the River Luineag at grid reference 937101 opposite the Moormore road, southwards towards the track junction nicknamed 'Piccadilly'.

This route was an old cart track. It is shown in the OS 6-inch map of 1902, except for a gap from the Rinraoich ruin to the next stream crossing. The section missing on that map is now on smooth grassland on freely drained soils. It is a fairly inconspicuous 'green road' with a surface mostly of grass. Probably in 1902 it continued across the gap, but so inconspicuous that surveyors presumably omitted it.

Luineag–Rinraoich

A 35-m length of track in native pinewood near the River Luineag had most of its loamy sand topsoil removed by a large tracked excavator or bulldozer in summer 1998 and deposited on the west side in a 7 x 4 m mound on top of classic Caledonian pinewood understorey of *Vaccinium myrtillus–V. vitis-idaea* with much *Rhytidiadelphus loreus* and *Hylocomium splendens*. Because no attempt was made to save the vegetation on the dump site before depositing the topsoil, the vegetation underneath will be killed. The soils at this site ranged from an imperfectly drained iron podzol next to the flush, to a freely drained iron podzol. The machine had skimmed off quantities of both, even though removal of the latter was unnecessary.

The next section took a line through a flush with tall rushes indicating nutrient enrichment, where the surface soil was a peaty gley resulting from a high groundwater-table. A slow streamlet ran across the track line. For a length of 20 m the machine operator had dug out all vegetation and organic soil down to a hard stony base, and dumped it along the sides of the track. No attempt was made to save vegetation before this dumping. Because the hard base lay well below the water level in the flush, the excavation created a pool up to 38 cm deep. Several exit drains had been dug by spade at the west side to lower the water level in this pool, but the gradient to the west is too slight in relation to water depth in the flush.

Hence the drains served little purpose, and were too short. Inspection of the small amount of growth in plants growing on the mostly bare excavated soils confirmed earlier evidence that the excavation had been done in July, about the middle of the month. Further south, the operator left minor signs of excavation on a short section.

Even if it were agreed that a track for land rovers should be allowed in this designated site, which seems dubious, it would have been wiser to have done no excavation with a big tracked machine, and used geotextile or other matting on the wet flush. This would have caused minimal damage to vegetation, soils, hydrology, and landscape. Moreover, it could have been removed if necessary after the event.

Rinraoich to second burn crossing

Many trees were cut, as described below under the heading Tree cutting in 1998. At the burn crossing, a large tracked machine had removed vegetation, organic soil, some subsoil, and boulders, along an 18-m length on the north side and 25 m on the south. The main surface soil in the area was freely drained fluvio-glacial sands and gravels, extremely so on the hillock beside the Rinraoich ruins, where patches of coarse sand had no vegetation. The sands and gravels overlie glacial till with a high content of clay. Close to the south side of the burn, the surface soil changes from fluvio-glacial to a peaty gley. Unfortunately the machine operator had cut down into the till on the south side. This left a steep gradient for the track on the south side, and small erosion rills were already apparent. Furthermore, the excavation into the till had resulted in locally unstable thixotropic conditions ('quicksand') in the clay, and much of this had been washed out by water erosion from the track down to a depth of 15 cm, and was discolouring the burn water.

Because the excavation has created a large deep open drain with no side drains to let water away, erosion will continue. Furthermore, the patches with thixotropic conditions extend throughout the width of the track close to where it adjoins the burn water. The result will certainly be removal of the thixotropic sections by water from the burn and the track, and this would be hastened by any further use of this burn crossing by vehicles.

Excavated boulders from glacial till were dumped on live vegetation near the burn, along with the organic top from the peaty gley and quantities of excavated vegetation including trees. The largest boulder was nearly 1 m in length. No attempt was made to retain vegetation, topsoil, and upper horizons of subsoil, or to reinstate the ground by putting these back carefully in reverse order. Some turves were lying upside down.

This crossing could have been developed with minimal impact by using geotextile matting, along with a ford of boulders and cobbles at a crossing point where the approaches were less steep and hence required less excavation or no excavation. It would have been useful also if consideration had been afforded to the use of a temporary bridge of girders for the vehicle wheels, as the burn is quite narrow slightly further upstream.

Second burn crossing to south end of tree cutting

A tracked machine had been used on the first part of this section to uproot several trees, and there were other minor signs of damage to vegetation. At one spot, a land rover had obviously become stuck, and had dug into the soft vegetation and soils. This left torn vegetation and soils, and standing water, with no attempt to reinstate the ground.. On another section with imperfectly drained soils, there were fairly long deep ruts on both sides, now filled with water, indicating where land rovers had repeatedly dug into the soft ground rather than taking nearby routes on firmer ground. Boulders, or preferably matting, would have prevented damage at both the above sites.

Some cut pine saplings had greyish-brown leaves, many of which had fallen off, indicating cutting prior to 1998. These had been thrown on to vegetation at either side, but cut stumps were on the track or at the very edge. The older cuttings did not extend north of the second burn crossing, and appeared in numbers only south of 933091 and increasingly further south as the track followed freely drained fluvio-glacial ground providing good driving. Where big saplings had been growing on the track in the north sections and would have been a barrier to a land rover or Argocat or other off-road vehicle, there was no sign of vegetation abrasion or other damage at the side, which would certainly have been evident if vehicles had made such detours in recent years or in 1998. This indicated that a) stalkers did the old tree cutting to keep the track free of trees, b) their main use of it was by land rover or other four-wheel drive vehicle from Piccadilly, not Rinraoich, and c) the main past use of the track was by land rover, not smaller all-terrain vehicles such as Argocats or low-pressure wheel bikes.

Tree cutting in 1998

The most southerly tree cutting in 1998 was at 934087. On our return walk on 15 October, we counted Scots pine trees cut in 1998, with one observer covering each side of the track from this southern point to the River Luineag near Rinraoich. The total was 719 pines and one juniper, including a few trees uprooted by an excavator or bulldozer. This number exceeded that noted on earlier inspection, probably because the dead trees were now more conspicuous than earlier, due to slow browning of the withering green pine needles, and also because the count on 16 October was by two observers. No other tree species had been cut.

The cut pines varied in age and height from five years old and 10 cm high, to 20 years old and 3 m high with basal diameter of 12 cm. The most rapidly-growing trees were putting on up to 35 cm of growth annually in recent years. Most were saplings, with almost no seedlings. In some places, so many had been felled that the cut trees lay on one another forming a low hedge on top of the heather, and would eventually kill the underlying vegetation by shading. No attempt had been made to spread such clumps out. Several cut trees had been thrown to lie against living trees. Not only trees on and immediately at the side of the track had been cut, but some further out to 2 m away on either side, which was unnecessary. Cutting and disposal had been quick and insensitive, with no care for the landscape, and some trees were projecting upwards close by the track, in a manner that increased their obtrusiveness.

Potentially damaging operations

SNH's list of potentially damaging operations (PDOs) within SSSIs shows that at least six such PDOs occurred along this track. Some did serious damage, and were carried out in a way that caused maximal impact with no reinstatement works.

C. Removal of tracks on Mar Lodge Estate

Length (km) of tracks removed by the National Trust for Scotland since 1996

	Removed to footpath width	Removed totally	Total
Beinn a' Bhuird	3.5	3.1	6.6
Glen Derry	3.2	0.0	3.2
Glen Luibeg	1.2	0.7	1.9
Glen Dee	1.2	4.6	5.8
Glen Geldie	3.5	1.3	4.8
Total	12.6	9.7	22.3

Note. A further 1.5 km S of Bynack Lodge were closed to land-rover use.

Technical notes on track removal at Glen Derry and Glen Luibeg, 2002

I took part in visits to both glens on 12 August with Police Constable Jim Wood and Ian Murray, both of Braemar Mountain Rescue Team, and on 20 August to Glen Luibeg with JW and NTS staff Alister Clunas, Peter Holden and Dougie Baird, accompanied for much of the field time on 20 August by the two workmen who had been doing the work with the aid of an excavator. The 12 August visit was arranged following a request by Ian Murray and Jim Wood of BMRT. For the 20 August visit I was asked to come by AC. My role on both visits was to inspect the works independently, make relevant impartial scientific and historical comments as well as practical comments as a former deer-gillie on Derry, and then technical suggestions for mitigating environmental impacts and maximising reinstatement success.

The main point of these notes is not to assign blame, but to learn lessons by recognising that a better outcome with less environmental impact and higher reinstatement success could have been achieved, and should be the prime aim in future works. It is especially important that this is done in an area such as the Cairngorms, which is internationally outstanding for its wilderness, wild landscape, wildlife and the public recreation that depends on these features.

Glen Luibeg. This track was not bulldozed by former Swiss owner Panchaud as at Beinn a' Bhuird, Quoich, Derry, Glen Dee, and Geldie, as is obvious from there being no spoil heaps, excavated boulders and debris. It was a cart track, as stated by Seton Gordon in the *Scots Magazine*, and as told to me by him and by stalkers whose memory went back to the late 1800s, and as seen by me since I first went there in 1939. The track as far as the stream-side copse half way up the glen has not changed since, apart from widening and erosion on the slope up the second hillock), and some bulldozing on a short section at the stream-side copse, where spates in 1956 and later years had eroded the track severely. The survey of bulldozed vehicle tracks that I carried out in 1981-82 for Grampian Regional Council's Department of Physical Planning shows bulldozing on that short section, but none elsewhere on Luibeg track.

In my paper, 'Paths and people in the Cairngorms' (1984, *Scottish Geographical Magazine* 100, 151–159), I stated (p. 159), 'S. Gordon and old people on Mar told me that in the 1900s, when the Mar Estate had a "watcher" at Corrour Bothy, the Lairig Ghru path from Derry Lodge up Glen Luibeg bad such a smooth surface of grit that a horse with a cart could trot on it.' By 1943, most of it had eroded badly, with many boulders sticking out of peaty morasses; and loose cobbles and gravel, so that it became a stream after rain. The only part that has kept its former quality is a short stretch of a well-drained hillock at grid reference 032935 near Luibeg. The hillock mentioned is the second one west of Luibeg and the stretch mentioned is the traverse round that hillock.

A photograph in W.A. Poucher's *A camera in the Cairngorms* (published 1947, based on a visit in spring 1946) shows two people walking side by side along a flat section just east of the slope up the second hillock, clearly on a wide cart-track. The next flat section from the top of that slope traverses for 200 m or more round the hillock, and is the part mentioned in the above quotation. It has remained in excellent pristine condition, and I always considered it an example of first-class construction and demonstrated it as such to visitors. It was still in the same pristine condition on 12 August 2002.

On 20 August I was surprised to see that this was not so, despite concerns expressed on 12 August. Instead, a narrow path had been created, with unnecessary environmental impact on soils and vegetation from a new ditch excavated along the uphill side. On 12 August I said to AC that the NTS was open to public criticism for damaging an old feature of historical interest. Later I asked for work to stop until we went on the review visit on 20 August, but work was not stopped.

The old track has been buried under boulders and soil along its entire surface and verges. No works were needed, other than minor treatment to reduce erosion on slopes and washed-out sections, and to re-define the main route there. The standard of work on the Luibeg path is poor, and reflects badly on NTS as landowner and manager. Some would regard what has happened to the formerly pristine section as tragic and perverse, and indeed a form of official vandalism.

My wife Councillor Jenny M.S.R. Watson (Vice Chairman of Aberdeenshire Council's Infrastructure Committee, which includes Planning) raised a further question, whether NTS applied for planning approval for an engineering operation at Luibeg or other track-removal sites. She recalls no such application being registered for Luibeg or elsewhere. It is undeniable that an engineering operation involving two workmen with a large excavator took place for weeks at Luibeg track. Engineering operations involving a large excavator occurred in the last two years also at east Glen Derry, beyond Geldie Lodge, and Beinn a' Bhuird.

Turves. On the Derry slope and at Luibeg, many heather turves had died or partly died. Excavated turves tended to be too small in area, especially those with tall heather, and had been removed along with too shallow a thickness of peat. Some had an edge drying out, because sand or gravel was not level with the turf's upper surface. Several were upside down and others sideways up. On the Luibeg path on 20 August, I pointed out one big turf lying completely upside down, and turned it over, but no NTS staff present said whether action would be taken on this.

At Derry slope and Luibeg, many wetland turves were on freely drained sites, and many from freely drained sites were in wet sites. I pointed this out to the party on 20 August at the Luibeg path. DB said that the workmen are asked to put turves on the relevant appropriate sites, but often dry and wet sites are close together. This explanation was inadequate. Freely drained versus poorly drained excavated sites are obvious from the vegetation immediately adjacent as well as from the soil that is being excavated. A frequent flaw with reinstatement works is that operators do a considerable amount of excavation, and turn to reinstatement as a separate procedure later. The best result comes from excavation and reinstatement of each short section as a combined unitary operation within a brief time, measured in minutes. If so, very little extra time is needed to do the best job, and mistakes involving depositing turves in the wrong sites are far less likely. It cannot be argued that this would have necessarily cost more money at Luibeg track. Indeed, much money could have been saved by avoiding cutting uphill ditches in fluvio-glacial material, beside big pine trees, and on other freely drained ground with no or virtually no catchment.

On many short sections of the new Luibeg path, plants do not demarcate the downhill edge. Turves should be put there to form a visual line for walkers and to trap gravel that otherwise will move to widen the path. If not, walkers may well tend to walk side by side on such short sections, causing further damage. On the Derry slope, turves should have been placed in a different pattern, to reduce erosion and increase colonisation by hill plants. By different pattern I mean that some areas of bare gravel on a fairly steep gradient were left too big and others unnecessarily small. The bigger bare parts should have had some turves inserted to act as small points for vegetation spread. On the steepest places, it would have been wise to insert such turves as far as possible longitudinally along the slope, to form terraces. This would reduce erosion risks greatly.

Tree roots and bark. On the 20 August visit, I said that I noticed on 12 August that pine roots had been cut carelessly by the excavator. NTS staff denied that this had happened, but later I pointed to roots that had been cut by major excavation at the pine copse halfway up Glen Luibeg, and living bark cut on one tree there. Severed roots should be covered with peaty soil, and the now unstable over-steepened bank should be treated. The bank requires to be put back approximately in its previous form. This damage is a result of applying the rule of excavating a ditch on the uphill side, even where, as here, it is unnecessary and indeed damaging.

Soils. Fertile upper horizons of subsoil (i.e. upper B) were generally not saved for reinstatement, thus wasting a valuable resource. In the Derry restoration along the slope, at one point the excavator had taken subsoil containing a high proportion of clay, and deposited it near the surface without leaving a finish of freely drained subsoil with its associated topsoil and vegetation. This is on a section with water flushing from higher up. The result is that thixotropic conditions have developed, i.e. a small quicksand. In other places at Derry slope, bare gravel on the surface should be raked to expose topsoil immediately below, and thus increase vegetation colonisation.

Soil material for path. On Glen Luibeg, much of the material used was fine fluvio-glacial sand. It has no binding quality, and especially when dry it is easily moved by walkers' feet and by bicycles. Due to lack of finer material between sand grains, it does not become appreciably firmer on compaction, and remains loose, thus being highly susceptible to water erosion and movement by people. We were informed by DB that this was the only material available. I advised that an exploratory survey should have been done at Luibeg and should be mandatory at future works, using a spade to dig small trial pits so as to look for better material. If this is not done, excavator drivers are likely to use whatever material is easily available on the first excavations, without wider checks. Since nobody present countered my suggestion by stating that such exploratory soil pits were dug at Luibeg, one can infer that none was done. I expressed concerns about the unsuitability of fluvio-glacial sand when we visited Mar Lodge at the end of the 12 August visit. It was noted on 20 August that the section most recently completed had a much larger proportion of fine dark material and hence would bind better on compaction and in rain. A reasonable inference is that this was done as a result of the concerns expressed about this topic on 12 August.

Path width and camber. JW was concerned about the final Luibeg width being less than 1 m in some places, too narrow for a wheeled stretcher. This would result in wheels sticking at times on vegetation at the side, thus jolting the stretcher and causing damage to plants. Using a tape at such places on 12 August, I measured the minimal width from one edge to the other (i.e. held vertically above the edges and thus not including any extra dimension due to the actual path surface where it was peaked in the middle). In the narrow places the measurements were fairly often down to 75 cm, and in one spot only 70 cm. These narrow sections were short, most of the path having a width of 1 m and in a few places slightly more. During the field part of the 20 August visit and at Mar Lodge at the end of it, DB maintained that the NTS had reasonably met their assurances to BMRT on path width, but this was manifestly not the case. In the end, DB accepted this at least implicitly, by agreeing to build the Luibeg path up to a minimum width of 1 m throughout.

JW had made concerns known about the camber of the finished Luibeg path, because a ridge had been created longitudinally along the path's central line, with fairly steep gradients down from it on both sides to the path edge. Obviously this would tend to shed water sideways and hence reduce erosion longitudinally along the line of the path. JW's concerns were that the peaked ridge would cause difficulties with the wheeled stretcher, and that tired walkers in poor light would be more likely to slip and fall because of the peaked ridge. There is no doubt that tired walkers in poor light find a flat cross-section easier, and my view is that the ridge is too peaked for easy walking. I found it so narrow and the slopes on either side so steep that I had to make a conscious effort to put my foot right on the central ridge, and any step to the side led to a slight jolt and a movement of surface gravel or sand sideways. DB thought that the peaked ridge would decrease in time, due to such movement and compaction, and to settling in rain. There is no doubt that the peak would decrease, but the time span before the path became fairly flat and lacking a peaked ridge is not definitely known. After concerns were made known about this on 12 August, it was notable on 20 August that the section done most recently lacked the high peaked ridge, and instead had a curved cross-section with a wider flat part on the top.

Drains. A ditch had been excavated on the uphill side throughout the length of the new Luibeg path and the south section that I visited on the reformed Derry path north of the footbridge at Derry Dam. Although such a ditch is standard practice on public roads and many new Scottish path-works, often it is not necessary, and indeed can be damaging on certain freely drained soils with some induration. In such cases it causes unnecessarily great environmental impacts and worse erosion. On freely drained fluvio-glacial hillocks as on part of the Luibeg path, especially those with a small catchment, there is no need to excavate a deep drain on the uphill side. Indeed, this concentrates run-off at one point and leads to erosion, and also damages soils and vegetation. It is worse if it cuts across an iron pan. At one burn crossing on the Luibeg path, east of the stream-side copse, the excavator had cut the iron pan and an indurated layer below it, at a point where the catchment uphill is lengthy and steep. I advised that boulders should be built up in the burn there, to a level just reaching above the cut iron pan, to prevent potentially serious erosion after heavy rain, At the Derry path, excavation of a ditch on the uphill side left a slope that was too steep and unstable at its uphill edge.

This has been followed by downhill movement of the soil and vegetation below, leaving a gap. Such a gap increases instability and will lead to further downward movement of soil and to water erosion. It should be in-filled.

In places where trees are growing, especially old pines with a big root network, the ground is particularly freely drained because of high evapo-transpiration, and drains on the uphill side are unnecessary and damaging (this comment applies to Luibeg and the Derry slope). In one place at the west end of the Luibeg works, a ditch had been excavated on the uphill side, even though the hillock above was almost flat and covered a very small area, had freely drained soil, and also supported old pines that would be removing much soil water.

Freely drained ground is obvious from its heather vegetation with some bell heather and reindeer lichen species characteristic of dry sites, whereas poorly drained ground is obvious in the Luibeg–Derry area from purple moor grass and deer sedge, or cotton grass on thick peat. It is surprising that evidently no cognisance was taken of such obvious differences.

Burn crossings. At Derry and Luibeg, these involve a large boulder set flat on one side of the burn, with the flat surface typically about a foot above the burn bed, a vertical drop down to the burn, and a narrow gap between the two boulders, thus allowing a walker to cross easily and dry shod. At bigger burns the gap is wider. One result is that the burn's flow is channelled more than before, and in future rainstorms there will inevitably be a faster flow and consequently more erosion at the downhill end of the gap. Also, a gillie would not lead a pony across such a gap, whether it was not laden or carrying a stag. Instead he would lead it round, above or below the step crossing, thus leading to more damage to vegetation and soils off the new footpath.

JW expressed concerns that the new crossings would be more difficult for rescuers moving a wheeled stretcher. He also thought there would be extra risk to walkers tripping by putting a foot into the gap, when soft snow covers the gap, and my view is that he is correct on this. Also I believe that the wide gaps pose a risk to cross-country skiers when soft snow fills the gaps.

JW had been given written assurances by NTS that the burn crossings on the Luibeg path would he suitable for a wheeled stretcher, with a shallow gradient on either side. When JW spoke of his concerns on this at Mar Lodge at the end of the 12 August visit, AC said they would ask DB to come down to have a look at the Luibeg ones. On 20 August, AC told me that on the NTS site visit with DB since 12 August, they immediately saw that the burn crossings were not as assured to JW, and all three NTS staff on the 20 August visit agreed with this. Since workmen had been operating on the Luibeg track for three weeks, no supervisory visit could have been made by NTS to check that workmen were respecting the contract specifications. Otherwise, such an obvious defect would surely have been noticed. A technically competent person ought to be with the workmen on the first day for at least the main part of that day, and should again be with them when a major change is anticipated such as the first burn crossing to be tackled.

On later reflection about the burn crossings, I suggest a change. The original wide shallow crossings could be left as they were. Walkers should not expect to cross without getting water on their boots. Big boulders forming steps look out of place in a semi-wilderness area such as Glen Luibeg. Standard practice for burn crossings on modern Scottish paths should not be obligatory for all areas, irrespective of altitude and snow-lie. Also, leaving the original wide crossings would allow rescuers to cross while having to lift the stretcher only slightly. The sole proviso I would suggest is that where a burn crossing has eroded the path on one side or the other, or has gouged out a deep rill or gully, measures should be taken to strengthen the edges of the path next to the burn, using boulders, and to fill the central channel of the burn at any crossing where the flow has gouged out a deep gully.

Water-bars. An example of a new one was shown on the slope up the second hillock on the Luibeg track. This would cause a small jolt with a wheeled stretcher. I suggested that cobbles and pebbles, interlocking to some extent if possible, be placed against the water-bar, to ease any jolting for the stretcher and reduce water speed along the bar. This was agreed.

Specifications for workmen. The above comments are so extensive that the question arises to what extent the workmen were given detailed specifications on the tasks. During the 20 August visit, one or other of the two workmen present was heard by me saying at three widely different sites "It's a pity we weren't told this at the start". Such comments by them might be regarded speculatively as attempts to absolve themselves from blame, but nobody present countered their comments, so it was evident that the workmen were genuinely not given sufficiently detailed instructions.

Big boulders. A few big boulders excavated on the Derry slope had rolled down and not been put back. They were obtrusive because of their pale weathered surface without rock lichen. If boulders are moved, those with rock lichen should be replaced right way up. Boulders without rock lichen should be buried and covered with subsoil, topsoil and vegetation. On the Derry slope above the footbridge, a large boulder had been dislodged slightly, leaving a gap of 5 cm behind it, and had not been put back. Such a boulder left in an unsafe position could move as a result of frost and rain, and cause injury.

Erosion rills. At one site on the Derry slope, a rill that had developed because of accelerated erosion from too large an expanse of bare gravel on a fairly steep gradient had seriously eroded a steeper slope below. This requires work to fill the rill with boulders. Also the cause requires treatment to reduce the extent of bare soil and stones higher up, to make turf terraces, and to reseed using a grass mixture of species native on Scottish moorland.

Litter and fuel drums. On 12 August, two fresh food-wrappers lay just outside the excavator door, and several full fuel drums stood on the ground nearby. The workmen and their van were not present.

Gravel washed from the planted wood. On the 20 August visit, I pointed to an expanse of gravel that had been washed recently down to the track's upper edge at a flat point between the first two hillocks, and asked if there was a drain in the wood. It seemed unlikely that so much gravel would wash out from an excessively drained fluvio-glacial hillock with many trees, unless water had been concentrated by a drain, perhaps dug unwisely and unnecessarily when trees were planted to augment natural regeneration. I recommend that a member of NTS staff should walk along the line of gravel uphill into the wood, to the gravel's source. If an old drain is there, it should be filled completely with cobbles and gravel, paying special attention to the top source.

Dr Adarn Watson, Centre for Ecology & Hydrology, Banchory AB31 4BW, 26 August 2002

D. Old Military Road, Corgarff, 2002–09

Inspection of engineering works, 3 July 2002

I carried out a brief inspection for less than an hour on the evening of 3 July. This involved being a passenger in a car driven slowly along the section that was altered by the works, and stopping at three places to walk and view ground more closely.

Engineering operations took place in early summer 2002. Some impacts of spoil deposition on vegetation were fresh, indicating deposition in May–June. The altered section of track starts south-east of Ordgarff, runs east in a coniferous plantation almost as far as Delachuper, goes on a plantation's south edge with moorland on the track's south side, and next a long part with open moorland on both sides, ending east of Delavine Burn at 283069 beside a track to Delavine. The altered track length exceeds 2 km.

The British Army constructed the original track as part of the old military road from Blairgowrie to Grantown. A plan by G. Campbell (1750) in the British Library (BL) is entitled Survey from the Water Aveun to Brae-marr Castle measuring 27 miles. A later BL plan is Plan of Part of the Road from Perth to Fort George between Braemarr and Corgarff Barracks, Made by 4 Companies of Col. Holmes's, 2 of Lord Geo. Beauclerk's, and 1 of Lt. G. Skelton's Regiments of Foot, in Summer 1753. Harry Gordon, Engineers. Indigenous local folk in the 1980s told me that the section at Delavine and Delachuper was The King's Road. A well known right of way, it features in several guide books.

The old track's width and surface are visible in two sites where recent engineering works were not done. The width of the driving surface of the newly engineered track (3.5 m) is about half as much again as the old width (2.4 m). The thickness of subsoil laid on the old track has obliterated it, except in the above two undisturbed sites. This affords a useful opportunity for comparison. Unlike the small interlocking dark stones forming a high proportion of the old track's surface, the new surface is of raw un-weathered subsoil, pale yellowish-orange in colour and obtrusive in the generally dark-coloured heather-dominated landscape. On the unaltered parts of the old track, grass and other plants cover much of the centre and sides, and even some of the running surface for wheels. This reduces erosion and renders the track unobtrusive. In contrast, the long newly engineered sections have no vegetation on their greatly widened surfaces.

The new surface's high content of clay, combined with compaction by 4 x 4 vehicles, is certain to result in soft surfaces and soil erosion during thaws and heavy rain. Already there are pot-holes and water pools on the surface, and small erosion rills. On part of the route, the surface shows that subsoil there was rolled when the stored material was wet. Near Ordgarff, freely drained gravel, darker in hue than the new road surface, has been dumped, evidently for top-dressing part of the road in the plantation.

On the west side of a ford at 272076 east of Delachuper, recent works involved re-routing to the south on previously unaffected ground. At the burn west of Delavine were deep marks of recent excavator tracks in the burn-side vegetation and soil, and excavation of the watercourse itself, leaving a-steep bank of exposed topsoil, almost vertical. The question arises whether SEPA was informed and gave permission.

Several borrow pits were excavated in hillocks to gain subsoil for spreading on the newly engineered and widened track. All excavated banks on the cut (up-slope) side were left too steep, and many are vertical or in places even slightly overhanging. This will lead to slope instability and extremely slow colonisation by vegetation, and minor collapses on the cut side have already occurred. Fill banks are mostly at lower angles and hence should be more stable and more prone to vegetation recovery. Since most of the cut was used for road metal, fill banks are fewer as well as smaller than cut banks.

A ditch was excavated along the up-slope side of the road's running surface for almost the entire length, irrespective of whether there is a perched water-table due to an iron pan or other induration, or whether there is a groundwater-table in peaty gleys or thick peat. The hydrological consequences of interrupting such water-tables, as distinct from merely diverting surface water, were ignored, and culverts had too small a diameter. Likewise, cut-off drains were excavated further up-slope in areas of flush vegetation indicating high groundwater-tables. The need for all this engineering work seems open to doubt. The question arises whether prior survey was done by a technically qualified soil scientist with practical expertise in hydrology, reinstatement, and road construction. Such survey certainly should have been done.

Apart from use of peat or topsoil to cloak almost all of the bare subsoil on excavated slopes of some borrow pits, reinstatement works have been inadequate if one aim was to minimise impacts and fit the track into the landscape. Many boulders and large quantities of subsoil have been deposited on top of vegetation. The treatment of turves with vegetation and topsoil was inadequate, with many turves upside down and others projecting into mid-air. Even where turves were placed right way up, the soil at the edges is exposed, which will lead to desiccation and plant death. A high proportion of the excavated heather turves had too shallow a thickness of peat or topsoil, and often too small a turf in surface area, resulting in much browning of foliage and a likelihood of plant death. At the burn just east of Delachuper, boulders were deposited in a steep pile on the fill slope, with no attempt to cover them with subsoil or topsoil and vegetation. Trees were unnecessarily damaged there by the excavator, and two excavated trees were dumped on the nearby hillside.

Given the big area of vegetation involved in track widening, cut slope and borrow pits, the amount visible on the surface is very small. The sole conclusion possible is that most of the affected vegetation was buried under boulders and subsoil. Had one aim been to minimise environmental impact and maximise reinstatement, vegetation with topsoil or peat should have been excavated carefully and stockpiled, and separately the upper horizons of subsoil, for putting back in reverse order..

To minimise impacts, engineering works should not be completed before reinstatement works begin. To ensure maximal reinstatement, the excavation and reinstatement should both be done each day, excavating the first section and then doing reinstatement on it that day, before moving to the next section. Clearly this was not done. Many heather turves were wasted by being placed with little care in the bottom of the cut slope (i.e. in what is effectively a drain), where much of the vegetation is likely to die and where the turves will lead to impeded drainage.

West of Delavine Burn the excavator driver had caused unnecessary ground damage away from the immediate culvert site, including leaving a hazardous wide hole almost a metre deep, and smaller holes.

The King's Road is a historic track 248 years old. It formed an interesting right of way for walkers and cyclists, with a good freely drained surface on a track that fitted well in its subdued dark hue and small width into the open moorland landscape. The newly engineered road is highly obtrusive in the landscape, being a wide conspicuous stripe of yellowish-orange subsoil, which makes it monotonously uniform for walkers or cyclists. Engineered cut banks, borrow pits, and dumped boulders and subsoil, along with culverts and marked reductions in road gradients due to extensive fill, add to the monotony and conspicuous obtrusion of the new track.

In short, recent engineering operations obliterated a historic trackway and resulted in a road which does not fit into the landscape. They resulted in material widening throughout the length, and re-routing at one ford. The design did not minimise the need for engineering and road-related earthworks (see Appendix below).

The entire track is in the area recommended by Ministers for the Cairngorms National Park. In such land of outstanding national and international importance, it is expected that planning authorities and individuals should take extra care, even though the Park is not yet designated. There are cases of good practice in Scotland where a new vehicle hill track or substantial upgrading was constructed with minimal impact, leaving no bare ground other than the narrow running surface. A photograph of such a track in the Lammermuirs has been published. The technical details how to do such work have been known to scientists for many years and are being applied by some contractors.

Appendix

A letter to me by Mr Hamish Porter of Aberdeenshire Council's Stonehaven office (31 January 2002), on the subject of a different track near Braemar, includes the following "The Planning Authority does not consider that maintenance of an existing track would require planning permission. The extension, alteration, re-routing or material widening of such a track would require planning permission for an engineering operation".

Aberdeenshire Council's Local Plan Policies, Finalised Draft, Appendix 1, 30 April 2002, Policy Env\23 on Vehicle Hill Tracks, includes the statement that vehicle hill tracks "must not obliterate existing paths and historic trackways, and their design should minimise the need for engineering and road-related earthworks".

Candacraig Estate damaged the 1700s Old Military Road at Corgarff, left an overhanging bank, almost all vegetation destroyed, many boulders not buried, unnecessary top drain, damaged area three times the width of running surface which was also unnecessarily wide, July 2002.

Site inspection 18 July 2002

A more detailed site inspection for half a day was made by Alexander D. Walker (former Principal Scientific Officer and officer in charge of the Grantown office of the Macaulay Institute for Soil Research) and A. Watson on 18 July. During this we gave technical advice to Aberdeenshire Council Planner Ms Aude Chabin (and briefly to shooting tenant Mr Robert Shields and head gamekeeper Mr Leslie George when they came past in a vehicle and stopped to speak with us). The main additional flaws noticed were:-

It was unnecessary to excavate the track surface to a far lower level on a hillock east of Delavine Burn, and to dig a deep open ditch on the uphill side, because soils there were freely drained. The ditch's gradient towards the burn was too steep and erosion had begun. The road camber on the section down towards the burn was in an unstable state and should be re-profiled.

All culverts were above the water-table, despite the wet summer, and should have been installed at a lower level. Moreover, no mesh screening had been inserted to prevent debris from filling and blocking culverts under the road.

The operator had ignored the need to have safe release of water on the down-slope, and scouring with erosion will be inevitable.

About half way along, where the road traverses a slope immediately above old fields, the fill bank had been left in a highly unstable state, the down-slope being far too steep and the subsoil too loose and freely drained. The track's down-slope edge had begun to fall away, and subsoil and stones to bury the fence below.

Alexander D. Walker & Adam Watson, July 2002

Notes on events at Corgarff in late 2002

Towards the end of the above site visit on 16 July 2002, Ms Aude Chaiban told Mr Shields and Mr George, in the hearing of three others (including Dr Adam Watson and Councillor Jenny Watson) that an unauthorised engineering operation had been carried out, so the estate would have to apply for retrospective planning permission. Neither Mr Shields nor Mr George refused.

After Dr Calum Campbell complained about the damage in a letter of July 2002 to local Aberdeenshire Councillor Bruce Luffman, the latter replied on 7 August, stating 'My initial reaction when I walked the whole road was that it was a well constructed new surface....Whilst I have a lifetime's interest in both historic sites and culture, I am still of the view that little or no long term damage has been done". In May 2003, Councillor Luffman became a member of the Board of the Cairngorms National Park Authority, and still was on the Board in 2003.

The planning service decided that a retrospective planning application would be required, in which case the Council could give permission, with attached conditions on reinstatement. On 7 September 2002, Ms Alyson James of the planning service wrote to Mike Rumbles MSP, stating that a letter had been sent to the estate's agents Savills, reiterating the view of the planning service 'that an application for planning permission should be submitted and that this would be the appropriate mechanism to resolve the remedial works which are required. Naturally, I hope to receive a planning application in due course, but should the Candacraig Estate decline to submit an application the Planning Service will have to give consideration to enforcement action'.

The estate then declined to submit an application, whereupon the planning staff considered dropping the option of enforcement action in favour of a voluntary agreement with the estate on reinstatement works. At a meeting at my house in December 2002, Ms Aude Chabain and a more senior planning officer Mrs Mary Macleod came to discuss the issues of reinstatement with me. Mrs Macleod clearly favoured agreement rather than enforcement. I countered this, because it would weaken the Council's resolve to take enforcement if the estate were to ignore some or all of the agreement. The two officers left with the option still undecided, but it appeared clear to me that Mrs Macleod as a senior officer would get her way. This proved to be the case.

On 20 November 2002, Ms Alyson James of the planning office wrote to Mike Rumnbles MSP, stating that a response had been received recently from Savills on behalf of Candacraig Estate. "They have indicated that they are willing to meet with Council Officers to discuss reparation works in relation to the track and adjacent land". However, the meeting did not take place until April 2003. In that month, Ms Chabain had a site meeting on the estate with the

Boulders left uncovered at Old Military Road, wide sections of bare gravel, almost no reinstatement, July 2002.

Savills factor Mr Robin Leslie Melville and the head keeper Mr Leslie George. Over the summer, she negotiated with the estate, aiming for reinstatement works that would be acceptable to the planning service. Meanwhile, the opportunity provided by another plant growing season was lost due to delay and inaction by the estate and the planning service.

When a local resident complained about the damage and the delay in a letter of June 2003 to CNPA Convenor Andrew Thin, he replied in July 2003 after consulting CNPA planning staff, "we are satisfied that the remedial works to be undertaken at Corgarff should achieve the same end result as that of undergoing a retrospective planning application or enforcement action".

On 22 August 2003, Mike Rumbles MSP sent a letter to a local resident who had complained about the damage to the road. He had received a letter from Mr Porter, Area Planning Officer (Marr). Mr Porter 'confirmed that the Planning Service is currently awaiting a submission from Candacraig estate of a schedule of works to be carried out of repairs/improvements to the road with a view to having the work carried out this year'. Mr Porter states that 'formal Enforcement Action is a matter of last resort and is taken entirely at the discretion of the Director of Planning and Environmental Services. The Council's remit is first of all to negotiate a voluntary resolution to the problem and in this case, through negotiation, the Estate has agreed to submit a schedule of works. If this is approved and carried out to the satisfaction of the Planning Authority then this would resolve the matter. This is apparently standard practice and Mr Porter does not believe that it creates any precedent, as the option is always kept open to take Enforcement Action if necessary'.

It should be noted that there was opposition within the planning service to this move, at least involving the archaeological staff (Ian Shepherd), as well as Mr Shaun Norman of the Inverurie office and Mr Allan Garvie the senior policy planner in Aberdeenshire Council. Nonetheless, because the development control section of the service was primarily involved, these concerns were ignored.

Ms Chabain sent a letter to me on 4 September 2003, stating that the estate proposed to carry out certain measures, and asking for my views on these. Mr Walker and I replied on 16 October (see our letter below). We had earlier stated on 5 August (Technical recommendations etc, below) that because the main plant growing season was now past for 2003, reinstatement works should be postponed until spring 2004.

Councillor Luffman spoke to AW and Dr Robert Moss at the Panmure Arms Hotel in Edzell before the first full CNPA meeting of 12 September 2003, which he attended as a Board Member. He said I would be pleased to know that the estate had decided to base its reinstatement on the recommendations by A.D. Walker and AW of 5 August 2003.

Mr Walker and I had expected a start to reinstatement works in spring 2004, but the estate informed Council planners that reinstatement would be done by the end of the 2004 planting season. Yet another plant growing season was lost. In fact, work did not start until summer 2005, three years after the damage and two years after Mr Thin's letter. By then, the optimum time for reinstatement had long passed. This exemplifies the inefficacy of voluntary agreements. Furthermore, it reveals the weakness and lack of grasp of reinstatement issues by Mr Thin and the CNPA planning staff in July 2003.

In *Mountain Views* (Autumn 2003, 14–15), an article on 'Controversy at Corgarff' by Jennifer A. Cook (Chairman of the North East Mountain Trust) was published, describing the damage done to the Old Military Road by Candacraig Estate. Also, an article by Dr Calum Campbell was published in *Leopard Magazine* (No. 297, 12–14, August 2003, 'Bell tolls for a historic road').

One of the main criticisms of the planning service over the Corgarff road in relation to other planning applications involves inconsistency and delay in decisions. In a case at Tillybrake in Banchory, a large company (Chap Construction Ltd) that was developing new housing made a small error about location in one housing block, whereupon a nearby resident complained about the new building being too near his house. The Council's planning service swiftly served an enforcement notice, and the company complied by demolishing the building and starting afresh with a new building that met the planning conditions. Likewise at an earlier case near Belts of Collonach at Strachan, enforcement action soon led to a new house being taken down and started afresh. The three years of delay at Corgarff and the failure to serve enforcement notice provide a revealing contrast with such cases. In 2005 I pointed out this inconsistency and contrast over the Tillybrake case in a BBC TV broadcast about unauthorised engineering operations on hill tracks at

Councillor Jenny Watson stands in unnecessarily deep drain at new works on Old Military Road, near-vertical bank, heather turf collapsed into drain, July 2002.

Invercauld, Dinnet and Corgarff. The inconsistency was manifest in the swiftly imposed enforcement notice by the planning service at Balmore, yet its absence in more than one track at Slugain and more than one at Dinnet.

An associated factor in this inconsistency and delay over tracks as compared with buildings is that there is a bias among planning officers and indeed the planning system as a whole towards emphasis on building control, with less emphasis and rigorous scrutiny over other issues such as forestry and tracks on hill land. Although the planning system dates from the Town & Country Planning Act of the late 1940s, the 'country' part is secondary in the attitude of planning staff generally.

A bias in the Corgarff case has on several occasions affected two local residents who had written letters to the planning service, requesting answers about the delays and seeking information about what was happening. They received no replies, even though they posted new letters after some weeks or months, so the regulations on the maximum delay for a response by the public service were evidently ignored.

Adam Watson in May 2006

The main alterations due to engineering operations at the Old Military Road

Material widening. Inspection of two re-routed parts (the east end and the west bridge) shows that the new road is about half as wide again as the former route.

Treatment of original road surface. Most of this has been covered deeply by subsoil. In two areas, however (the hillock at the east end and the slope east of Delachuper), the original surface has been destroyed by excavating to a lower level. At some locations it has been disturbed by excavation to insert culverts.

New length of road. At the burn crossing east of Delachuper, a new route has been excavated south of the existing route, to prevent vehicles grounding. This could have been avoided by placing flat boulders in the burn to make a higher paved crossing.

Up-slope banks. These were excavated too steeply to hold vegetation, and will slip and erode as has occurred over the past year. Many are vertical, even overhanging in some places. Drains have been dug unnecessarily in freely drained soils, leaving their associated up-slope banks too high.

Old drains. Stone rubble drains inserted in wet up-slope flushes have been cut by excavator, leaving the cut ends exposed. The former paved cross-drains which traversed the road surface and connected with the rubble drains have been covered in subsoil and are no longer visible. It is likely that most were destroyed when excavating to insert culverts.

Down-slope banks. Much of this consists of stony coarse-textured subsoil including many boulders, and is inimical to plant colonisation. Some parts present a steep face of bare subsoil up to 40 cm high. Along the top edge of a field, the road has been taken too far on the down-slope, resulting in a deer fence being displaced.

Excavated vegetation, topsoil and peat. There should have been a big surplus of such material useful for reinstatement, but most of it has been lost by burial under infertile subsoil and boulders. A high proportion of the excavated turves that remained on the surface were left upside down or lying sideways, with the roots exposed. Different soil horizons were not stored separately and not replaced in the correct order.

Excavated boulders. Most were deposited indiscriminately, often on top of vegetation or topsoil. Many were dumped in prominent positions, such as at the bottom of the down-slope in the wood. Where large boulders formerly projected above the ground surface, frequently they were excavated and deposited with the conspicuous lichen-free pale surface uppermost and the dark weathered surface underneath or sideways.

Excavations and drains in freely drained soils. Some areas displayed freely drained soils with associated heather-dominated vegetation. There was no need to cut deeply into such soils or to create a deep drain to standard depth along the up-slope of the road. Excavations have cut through the iron pan, resulting in increased water flow during heavy rain from the hill on to up-slope excavated banks and into the drains. This will induce greater soil erosion and slippage.

Culverts. Most were inserted above the regional ground-water-table. Some had an inadequate drain, and some exits are in unsuitable locations likely to lead to increasing erosion.

Alexander D. Walker and Adam Watson, 5 August 2003

Soil scientist Sandy Walker shows soil features to local resident Jenny Smith, Councillor Jenny Watson and planning officer Aude Chabin at Old Military Road, July 2002.

Technical recommendations on reinstatement at the Old Military Road

The following are the measures that are required for minimal reinstatement:-

Up-slope banks. These should be re-graded to a gradient of not more than 30 degrees, using the surplus soil already deposited above the upper edges of the old faces. The new faces should be cloaked with turves and topsoil (or peat in wet parts), to hasten colonisation by hill vegetation and to reduce erosion. Where there is insufficient turf and topsoil (or peat), peat should be used from outwith the road site.

Down-slope banks. Boulders and stones should be removed to borrow-pits, and topsoil or peat replaced along with turves. Any outer face of steep subsoil should be consolidated by reducing its gradient and cloaking with topsoil and turves. The road's outer edge along the top of the field should be corrected by re-positioning the edge further south and removing the large boulders.

Borrow-pits. These should be re-graded, using an excavator to bury large boulders at the base, covering them with subsoil and topsoil cloaked with turves.

Scattered boulders. These should be gathered and buried in the borrow pits.

Placing of turves, topsoil and peat when cloaking subsoil banks. During excavation, much of this potentially rooting material was lost by burial. Where there is insufficient to cloak the entire surface of subsoil, such material should be dispersed in small patches. Turves that are upside down or lying sideways should be re-placed with roots facing down. Any living vegetation would then survive better and the seed-bank in the plant litter would enhance colonisation by vegetation. There is no need at this low sheltered site to use grass seed and fertiliser, as such measures would lead to an unnatural green strip through the heather and associated moorland plants.

Cross-drains. On wet sections, stones should be used to create rubble drains across the road, preferably consolidated and strengthened by an underlay of terram fabric.

Road camber. On the slope at the eastern end of the excavated part, the camber should be heightened on the up-slope side to reduce road-surface erosion.

Culverts. The construction of some culverts has led to ponding, and in some other cases to the culvert base being too high, sitting above the ground-water-table in summer. In the worst cases, the culvert should be reinstated at a lower level. A mesh screen should be inserted at the upper end of each culvert, to prevent the entrance becoming clogged with soil and plant debris.

Deep hole. A 1-m deep hole excavated in peat on the up-slope west of the middle bridge is a hazard and should be filled with peat. Inspection should be made to ensure that no other such holes remain.

Because the main season of plant growth for 2003 is now past, the above measures should be postponed until spring 2004.

Alexander D. Walker and Adam Watson, 5 August 2003

Letter of 16 October 2003

Aude Chaiban
Planning & Environmental Services
Aberdeenshire Council
Viewmount
Stonehaven

Dear Aude

Old Military Road, Corgarff

We have reviewed the estate's proposals as described in your letter of 4 September. It is unfortunate that, following the estate's agreement with you in April, it has taken so long for them to produce the proposals, thus losing the entire growing season. The measures that we recommended to you during the site visit in July 2002 would almost certainly have led to a satisfactory condition by now, had they been implemented in spring 2003. The estate's proposals are less detailed than the minimal reinstatement measures recommended by us in a note on 5 August 2003 and hence less satisfactory, even though we agree with most of them in principle. The following comments involve issues raised on page 2 of your letter, apart from our last comment below, which refers to the second bullet point on your page 1.

Councillor Jenny Watson stands in borrow pit used for surfacing Old Military Road, many boulders not covered, vegetation destroyed, pit poorly reinstated, July 2002.

There is evidently some misunderstanding about rubble drains. Our comment about these referred to point 5 in our 5 August note "The main alterations etc". The works in 2002 cut across the original rubble drains made in the 1750s on the uphill slope, leaving the cut ends exposed. Formerly, each of these rubble drains led into a paved drain across the road surface and thence on the downhill side to a safe exit. However, as a result of the 2002 works, water flow that is concentrated by these rubble drains now falls vertically into the new roadside ditch on the uphill side or on to the steep new uphill bank, and is liable to cause erosion. To solve this problem, one could fill the ditch with boulders and smaller rocks to form a French drain, and extend the original rubble drains from their cut ends down to the top of the French drain.

You write that rubble drains tend to be blocked by silt and require regular cleaning, and that a French drain would quickly fill with silt. None of the rubble drains made in the 1750s show blocking by silt and none has required cleaning; indeed they were underground. It is highly unlikely that silt would block a French drain in that location, because there would be insufficient water to mobilise enough silt to cause such blockage.

The comment that culverts were above the groundwater-table to prevent silt pollution of the river is of dubious validity. Our above statement about silt mobilisation being very unlikely applies also to culverts. The main flaw in the new down-slope exits is that most of them were poorly located. They should have been sited in safe locations where run-off and erosion were inherently less likely because of the topography and where the hollows below the exits were properly armoured. Any increase in sediment load (not just silt, but also finer and larger particles) into the river is more likely to result from poor exits than from culverts below the water-table.

We agree with your engineers that the ultimate engineering solution on drainage would be very expensive, but reiterate that the measures we recommended are reasonable and practical. Had the estate applied for planning permission and had this been granted with such provisos, many of the problems would have been less serious and would have required less attention and expense.

Geo-textile or netting on the steep banks would increase the speed of vegetation recovery and reduce erosion. However, this is not a site where erosion poses serious problems such as exist on the very long steep slopes at Cairn Gorm or on bulldozed tracks that climb a relatively steep gradient. The Corgarff road, in contrast, traverses a slope at roughly the same altitude. Also, the altitude is not high and the location quite sheltered. Hence, although netting would reduce the visual impact sooner, it is not necessary, because a start to vegetation recovery and major reduction of erosion are certain if the bank gradients are reduced as recommended by us.

Likewise there is no need to "Re-seed all exposed surfaces with heather seeds harvested on the adjacent moor" (estate's proposal in your second bullet point). Provided that bank gradients are reduced, boulders removed, and turf and topsoil/ peat used as in our recommendations, vegetation cover at this low altitude is certain. There is no good reason for such re-seeding merely to speed up the eventual cover of vegetation. Even if all bare surfaces were treated with heather seeds, a high proportion of seeds would not germinate because of the hostile conditions. Because the road-works involved large-scale wastage of the available vegetation and topsoil/peat, the bare stony infertile subsoil which forms most of the banks are not comparable with typical hill soils that are colonised by heather seedlings. Mosses, liverworts and lichens would be early colonisers of the bare subsoil, and would act as a nurse, creating conditions more suitable for heather. In addition, the heather varieties that would be most viable vary considerably according to the surface soil, including its moisture, and the exposure. Such variation in the type of heather colonist will occur if there is natural colonisation, whereas harvesting and seeding are unlikely to provide such a complex pool of heather varieties. Finally, harvesting and seeding would be expensive, and in our view neither necessary nor justifiable. Your engineers' statement about the ultimate drainage solution being very expensive and your response that this would not be justified, apply also to the estate's proposed solution on vegetation restoration.

Yours sincerely

Alexander D. Walker & Adam Watson

Note on events at the Old Military Road since 2003

Instead of starting work in spring 2004, Candacraig Estate did not begin reinstatement work before the end of June 2004, thus missing yet another main growing season (this is over by the end of June for moorland plants, late summer being mainly a period of seed production and increased fibre content of shoots.

On 30 July 2006, we walked the road from Delachuper to the bridge across the burn west of Delavine, to inspect the reinstatement. We were in a party of 18, mainly from the Council of the North East Mountain Trust, but including three residents from Strathdon, the convener of the Badenoch & Strathspey Conservation Group, a staff officer from the Cairngorms National Park Authority (CNPA), and one from SNH.

The only reinstatement in late summer 2004 was 1) some grass reseeding on the uphill spoil, and 2) removal of some boulders from the uphill spoil and their deposition in two borrow pits, one past Delachuper and one the east section near Delavine. Boulders were left on the flat base of the pits, without cover of soil or vegetation.

In fact, all but two recommendations have been ignored, and our recommendation about boulders was only partly implemented. The recommendation involved removal of boulders on the downhill side of the track as well as the uphill side, and their deposition in borrow pits with soil and vegetation cloaking the boulders.

It would be counter-productive to interfere with the banks, now that a considerable amount of colonisation by hill plants has taken place. The best time for this was years ago, immediately after the engineering works or early in the next growing season. However, obvious problems are now clearly evident with culvert entrances and exits, and occasionally along the edge of the road on the downhill side where an incorrect camber induces water to erode the downhill bank. It would be in the estate's interest to pay attention to these problems. Also, given the historical importance of the road, it could be useful to do some aesthetic works with the aim of improving the immediate view of the road for users. Such works would involve the removal and concentrated deposition of more boulders, and the cloaking of them with soil and vegetation taken from close nearby. We could provide detailed technical advice on this, if requested.

Alexander D. Walker and Adam Watson, 31 July 2006

Since the above, Mairi Stewart of the Planning Service at Stonehaven sent a letter on 5 September 2006 to Mike Rumbles MSP, informing him that a further visit to the road is required by the Planning Inspector, to 'check on the progress and subsequent establishment of the works and whether they have been carried out in accordance with the approved schedule of works and to the satisfaction of the Council'. In summer 2007 she informed Adam Watson and local resident Ms Jenny Smith that a site visit was planned for early autumn 2007, to assess the status of the repair works. Neither AW nor Ms Smith has been informed since then whether a visit took place, and, if so, what the outcome was. Ms Smith wrote on 15 June 2008 to Mike Rumbles MSP, hoping that the Planning Service would pay more attention to a representation by him. She added that in late summer 2007 an excavator cleared the ends of the plastic culverts and dumped the resulting small pockets of soil on to the bank, thus increasing the impact yet again. She thought that it should have been easy to put the spoil in a trailer and use it to cover some boulders in borrow pits.

E. Balmore and Slugain tracks, Invercauld

Technical observations on the widened Balmore–Auchtavan track, 2005

A site inspection was made on 18 November 2005, as far as 210955 at the first stream on the last level section towards Auchtavan. The following observations were made approximately in the order in which one views the track while walking from the bridge past Balmore.

Where the bottom of the track to Auchtavan turns west at 217944 beyond the bridge, a new track has been excavated to the east at approximately the same period as the one to Auchtavan.

Bare soil deposited on the down-slope side of the track to Auchtavan has been reseeded along a short section uphill from the bridge, and new grass covers a minor proportion of the bared ground. Given the large excess of vegetation and topsoil that are available when a track is made or widened, as here, there should have been no need for reseeding, which in any case is an unsatisfactory method. No reseeding is evident on the rest of the route.

A ditch has been excavated along the whole length of the track as far as 210955, on the up-slope side. On sections with freely drained soils at a low gradient, such a ditch was unnecessary. It has been dug unnecessarily deeply, generally about 1m but in some sections up to 2 m. The back wall of the ditch was left too steep along almost the whole route, almost vertical, and occasionally overhanging. On the first part of the track uphill from the bridge, the gradient of the uphill slope is steep, and the slope about 3–5m up shows a series of lengthy longitudinal cracks, some up to 30 m long and others only a few metres, marking previous slope collapses. The deep, highly friable nature of the A and B soil horizons on this colluvial slope adds to the likelihood of such collapses. The excavation of a deep ditch below these, with a vertical unstable back wall, brings the potential for more collapses on a larger scale.

Spoil from the excavator bucket was deposited in many places along the vegetation on the lip of the vertical edge above the ditch, killing the vegetation and causing further loose unstable conditions. In the many places where the up-slope bank above the lip was left unstable and loose, it would have been useful to knuckle the bucket on to the bank, so as to reduce the likelihood of frost, rain and gravity moving the loosened material.

The inward ditch at irregular intervals is filled virtually to the top with soil, stones, boulders and turves that have come down in the weeks since the excavation. Above the south bends, the track at 215950 leads through heather at a gentle gradient, almost level. There was no need to excavate a ditch there, and the excavated spoil was deposited on the up-slope side on top of the vegetation, occupying a band about twice the width of the ditch. There was no need to kill so much vegetation in this way.

In one section, a small natural drainage channel up-slope has disgorged water on to the vertical face and subsequently eroded it, filling the ditch completely at that point. Other natural drainage channels have been allowed to come straight on to the vertical face, cutting into it and undermining turves so that the bank is undercut with turf overhanging in mid air and likely to fall into the ditch. Natural drainage channels have been excavated in such a manner as to leave them as small waterfalls 1–2m high, devoid of any attempt to armour the up-slope back wall or make horizontal steps to reduce water speed. At one point above the south bend, a natural drainage channel has been concentrated by other excavations and by cutting a new straight line for the channel. This is unstable, and at its exit is already eroding the back wall. It has the potential to break through at a higher level, taking a more natural route straight downhill.

The cross drains consisting of plastic pipes are devoid of traps on the up-slope side and erosion spilling on the down-slope side. At most of the entry points on the uphill side, about half of the volume at the top end of the pipe was already in-filled with soil and stones. Some of the pipe exits debouch on to open slopes where erosion is likely to be more serious, and few of them lead into safe natural drainage channels. One exit had flat stones placed immediately below on the down-slope side, thus acting to reduce splash and erosion, but this was an exception. At the third cross pipe about 200 m up the track from the middle gate and before the south bend, the exit pipe leads natural stream water on to exposed subsoil at either side, immediately below the track's steep down-slope bank. This should have been continued in a plastic pipe for 20 m downhill to end on grassland in a natural drainage gully. The pipe below this one has an exit straight on to an open steep slope, and water is already spreading out laterally downhill. Every exit should be carefully chosen to end in a down-slope natural gully.

Excavator used for track from Balmore to Auchtavan, Invercauld Estate, August 2005.

Kenny Ferguson stands in unnecessarily deep ditch at Balmore track, gravel bank too steep, boulders not covered, August 2005.

Near-vertical bank of till shows gouges by excavator bucket, Balmore track, August 2005.

Boulders dumped on edge of Balmore track, August 2005.

Balmore track adversely affects fine views of Lochnagar; too wide road, uphill ditch, cut, fill, and downhill drain, August 2005.

Uphill culvert pipe on Balmore track almost blocked by eroded soil, 21 October 2007.

Downhill culvert pipe on Balmore track washed eroded soil on to unsafe exit of vegetation with no splash boulders and no natural watercourse, pipe left uncovered, 21 October 2007.

Periodically the up-slope ditch ends at a drainage pipe that crosses under the road, and for 1–3 m the excavator driver had left a gap without a ditch, thus forming a barrier to water coming down the ditch. This reduces the likelihood of a flood breaking through into the next section of ditch downhill. However, it is unsafe to turn water suddenly through a right angle without armouring the barrier with boulders. This was not done.

Some erratic boulders were left in an unstable position near the edge of the vertical back wall, and are now more likely to become loosened in thaws or rain, and then to roll down on to the road, posing a risk to people on the road. Many big roots of trees were cut during the ditch excavation, increasing the likelihood of treefall and further bank instability.

At the sharp bend at 212950, two box drains should have been inserted to remove surface water coming down the track. The lack of these has already led to erosion rills along the track surface for up to 150 m down the track, and most of the eroded material has ended in the ditch. In this upper section, where soils tend to be wetter because of flushes of spring-water, there have been partly successful attempts to intercept and remove slope water, but no attempt to reduce and remove water on the track surface. Above the bend, an exacerbating feature is that a large expanse of bared ground has been created, due to the excavator being allowed to travel too freely, without proper channelling. The extra bare ground inevitably leads to increased run-off and erosion, now posing threats to the track surface and the efficacy of the drains.

Unnecessarily large areas were used for numerous borrow pits. No attempt was made to reinstate the ground at these. No vegetation and topsoil were kept for eventually covering the exposed subsoil and conspicuous unweathered lichen-free boulders. This was also the case along the entire route of the track, where the large surplus of excess vegetation and topsoil has disappeared, presumably underneath the subsoil and boulders dumped on the downhill side below the track.

At the upper bend at 215000, the former track going eastwards and then turning north to Loin and beyond has been widened and upgraded at least for the first section visible from the bend, in the same manner and at about the same time as the main track to Auchtavan. At least the first 200 m had been altered, so this also should have been the subject of a planning application, along with the new track heading east from the bottom bridge.

Around the top bend and beyond on both sides of the track to Auchtavan, large numbers of birch trees have been felled and others killed by excavation, and the dead trees now lie dumped in several places. The purpose of this destruction is presumably to extend the moorland.

On the upper section where the track levels at about 213952 there are several sumps or hollows in the road. Water is likely to stay in these for considerable periods after rain or thaws. It would have been easy to level these off by depositing excess spoil from the borrow pits on these sumps, instead of dumping it on the down-slope side of the track where it performs no useful function. Using a trailer to remove such excess to the sumps would not have taken materially more time than dumping it here and there on the down-slope side of the track. In some places the width of unusable extra bare ground is as wide as the track itself. There is clearly a mismatch between far too much being removed from borrow pits and the much smaller amount that was actually needed. In short, the amount of engineering and earthworks greatly exceeded what was necessary, and this caused unnecessarily large impacts on soils, vegetation, and water systems.

Observers were a) Alexander D. Walker, former officer in charge of the Grantown office of the Soil Survey of Scotland (Macaulay Institute for Soil Research), b) Rodney E.F. Heslop also a former officer of the Soil Survey of Scotland, and c) Adam Watson, Emeritus Fellow of the Centre for Ecology & Hydrology at Banchory. ADW and REFH are retired soil surveyors, each with a lifetime of experience of Scottish soils. AW surveyed vehicle hill-tracks in north-east Scotland for Grampian Regional Council's Physical Planning Department in 1984, and has recorded new tracks since.

Addendum on Reporters' decision on Balmore-Auchtavan track, 2005

Technical comments on the decision letter of 22 September 2005. The numbers below refer to those in the decision letter.

17. The Appeal stated that 'requiring removal of all imported material is excessive. The resulting damage would be greater than the works carried out'. This last sentence is ignored in the Reporter's comments, which might imply that he

Downhill culvert pipe on Balmore track has unsafe exit on steep vegetation, 21 October 2007.

Kenny Ferguson of North East Mountain Trust at Balmore track uses a device to show maximum stable angle (c30 degrees gradient) that was made a condition by Aberdeenshire Council but ignored by Invercauld Estate, 1 March 2009.

Kenny Ferguson stands in centre of a borrow pit for Balmore track, 21 October 2007.

accepts the argument. In fact, the argument is fallacious. Although reinstatement is most successful when carried out during construction, even at a later date it always results in less impact than where reinstatement was mostly ignored as at Balmore-Auchtavan.

36. (a) It is invalid for the Reporter to conclude that the works constituted a permitted development. Likewise, it is not credible to assert that the works were carried out on agricultural land forming an agricultural unit, and likewise (c) that the 'works are requisite for the purposes of agriculture within the agricultural unit'.

The person who authorised and paid for the works, and who appealed against Aberdeenshire Council's enforcement notice was the shooting tenant who rents Invercauld House and the shootings of Glen Feardar. The Invercauld factor, Simon Blackett, is in charge of letting the sheep-grazing on the hill ground, and neither he nor the grazing tenant was involved in authorising and funding the engineering works, or in appealing against the enforcement notice.

In addition, sheep grazing on Invercauld generally has declined greatly since the 1950s, as is evident from the considerable natural regeneration of birch, willow and pine on open moorland, to the extent that the woodland as marked on Ordnance Survey maps now covers a larger area. One of us (AW) carried out a detailed survey of this natural regeneration in 1985, and plotted it on 1:10 000 OS maps, copies of which can be made available for consultation. There is now a very low density of sheep in summer, and none in winter, on all the hill ground of Glen Feardar and the neighbouring Gleann an t-Slugain, Monaltrie Moss and the moorland beside the Crathie-Gairnshiel road.

Indeed, the estate policy under Mr Blackett as factor has been to persuade farm tenants to reduce sheep numbers on the hill. In Glen Shee, this involved widely publicised threats to evict tenant Mrs Jean Lindsay at Runavey, which were challenged by the National Farmers' Union and led to a case accepted by the Scottish Land Court until the estate made an out-of-court settlement. The tenant at Broughdearg was pressurised to remove sheep from the hill, and Lovat Fraser the tenant of Old Spittal has removed his sheep from Gleann Beag. The estate persuaded sheep tenant of Glen Clunie, Mr Smith of Spyhill and Auchallater, to put sheep on Glas Maol and the Cairnwell hills for a much shorter period in summer, and also the total number of sheep on the hill has declined.

The Appeal claimed that the works were 'providing access to agricultural land and farm buildings'. There are no farm buildings at Auchtavan, yet the Reporter ignores this, even though the fact clearly demonstrates the invalidity of the quoted phrase in the Appeal.

The Appeal adduced no evidence for the assertion that the track had become rutted 'by heavy agricultural vehicles'. Presumably, the Reporter either accepted or ignored this lack of evidence.

48. (a). The Council's Plan sought 'integration into the landscape, with alignments that follow existing contours and fit in with landforms and landscape features'. The Reporter claims merely that 'With respect to landscape features, the birch wood through which the track passes serves to screen its appearance from the surrounding countryside'. This is not entirely accurate and is somewhat misleading because the wood does not screen it well in October–May when the trees lack leaves, and even in summer the track is still visible. Moreover, the Reporter ignores the impact on landscape for people using the track. He also ignores the question of 'integration into the landscape', and merely discussed the later phrase 'fit in with....landscape features'. The Reporter's assertion that 'Its appearance from the viewpoint at Balmore is not unacceptably prominent' is merely his subjective opinion. The phrase 'not unacceptably prominent' is an example of bad English. The Reporters Unit should strive for a higher standard of presentation.

49. Here the Reporter makes the surprising claim that 'there is no evidence to demonstrate that the works as carried out have created a feature that will in future be vulnerable to soil erosion or will be detrimental to the environment in some other way.' This indicates that the Reporter has a very poor understanding of the technical issues. His own point 3, describing his site visit, notes that 'On most of the north-east or uphill side of the track a drainage ditch has been excavated, creating in a number of places a near vertical exposed face of subsoil generally not more than 1 m in height'. His own point 4 notes that compared with the short unaltered section near Auchtavan 'the altered section of track is now double this width'. Given this doubling of the width of bare ground, the excavation of near vertical exposed subsoil and drainage ditches, the deposition of excavated subsoil on to steep downhill banks, and the general lack of any attempt at ground reinstatement, serious erosion of soil was inevitable. This has led to the deposition of silt and coarser sediments in the ditches, and erosion of the track surface. On our site inspection in November, serious erosion

Track by Invercauld Estate up the burn west of Meall Glasail Mor, Gleann an t-Slugain, unstable overhanging bank, cut tree-roots, boulders and gravel and silt into burn, no covering of boulders or ground reinstatement, most vegetation destroyed, 24 August 2007.

At south end of excavated track west of Meall Glasail Mor; heather dead because turf cut too shallow, 4 December 2001.

Steep unstable bank on excavated track west of Meall Glasail Mor, almost all vegetation destroyed and no reinstatement, August 2007.

Minor engineering at end of excavated track west of Meall Glasail Mor, 24 August 2007.

Logs at wet patch north of excavated track west of Meall Glasail Mor, 4 December 2001.

Minor engineering 600 m north of excavated track west of Meall Glasail Mor, looking towards Gairn, 4 December 2001.

Wheel tracks to grouse-butts beyond the excavated track west of Meal Glasail Mor and carrying on above butt and heading leftwards to top of Carn na Craoibhe Seileich, Gleann an t-Slugain, August 2007.

Former path in main Gleann an t-Slugain destroyed by excavated new track, December 2001.

Former path destroyed by excavated track in main Gleann an t-Slugain, further up, December 2001.

High east track in Gleann an t-Slugain, former footpath widened by vehicles and minor engineering, 25 September 2004.

had already taken place, and was visually obvious, including surface rills on the track itself. If turves, humus and upper horizons of mineral soil had been properly excavated, stored, and replaced in reverse order, there would have been no bare subsoil on uphill banks, downhill banks and borrow pits. Also the track could have been greatly reduced in width, especially at the bend where the track turns eastwards.

50. The Reporter asserts 'that the works have not entailed a greater degree of engineering or earthworks than is reasonably necessary'. This again shows surprising unfamiliarity with good practice. Most of the engineering and earthworks was unnecessary, and indeed unnecessarily expensive to the client. Because on most sections of the uphill side the soils are freely drained, there was no need to excavate such large deep ditches along the length of the new track. A ditch draining each wet and flushed site, connected to a drain across the track and leading to a safe exit on the downhill side, was all that was necessary.

51. 'My conclusion in relation to the finalised local plan is that the works are generally in accordance with what Policy Env\23 seeks to achieve'. This is a bald statement without any substantive evidence. It may be regarded therefore as a subjective opinion from someone who apparently lacks experience in the subject of tracks.

52. The Reporter claims 'No details of the features of an alternative design have been put forward by the Council and it is not clear to me to what extent the works could have been modified to reduce their impact while achieving their purpose'. It is surely up to a developer to put forward an appropriate design. If Council planners do not accept this, negotiation follows, aimed at producing an alternative design more likely to be approved. The report of our site visit shows that the works could have been done in a way that would reduce impacts greatly and maximise reinstatement. The Reporter stated earlier that the new track was double the width of the old (including ditches and deposition on banks). Hence, there should have been a large surplus of vegetation and topsoil, enough to cloak all subsoil on banks and borrow pits. Most of this surplus was destroyed by careless work, but a planning application with a method statement could and should have included this as a crucial objective.

53. 'SNH states that, had it been consulted at the outset, it would have recommended submission of a detailed method statement and specification to ensure that the track was appropriately constructed. I have noted that SNH does not say that the works that have been carried out are inappropriate, nor does SNH say that the impact that has occurred would be acceptable if disturbed areas were vegetated'. However, SNH must have considered the works inappropriate and the impacts unacceptable, otherwise it would be illogical of SNH to recommend a method statement. Because no reasonable impartial person could decide otherwise, it would appear that the Reporter shows bias. His phrase about disturbed areas being vegetated begs the question, for, as made clear above, all disturbed areas would have been vegetated had the works been done properly. This should have been an important part of a method statement in the planning application.

54. Here, the Reporter repeats his conclusion 'that it has not been demonstrated that the purpose of the works could have been achieved in a manner that would have had a significantly reduced impact on their surroundings, and that the impact that has occurred would be acceptable if disturbed areas were vegetated'. This statement is incorrect and misleading, as explained above, because all disturbed areas could and should have been vegetated with existing vegetation and topsoil if there had been a planning application and subsequently a negotiated method statement agreed with SNH and Council officers. These repeated conclusions of the Reporter manifest a deep ignorance of the technical aspects of the subject, and of normal good practice.

55-58. The Reporter again reveals a lack of understanding by setting such high importance on the reseeding of disturbed areas with grass seed and making this his sole condition for planning permission. The condition requires the developer to provide to the planning authority within two months, details on seed species, rate of seeding per unit area, ground preparation before seeding, steps to ensure establishment, steps to make good any areas where seeding fails, and the timing of the foregoing work. It should be recognised that no reseeding is necessary in this location at such a low altitude in a sheltered wood, and that, as shown above, development should have resulted in no bare subsoil and a surface completely vegetated with existing turf.

60. (2). 'No details of seed species have been provided and it is important to ensure that the species planted are appropriate to the locality. It is also important to ensure that an adequate quantity of seed is planted'. This stipulation illustrates again the profound lack of understanding of the subject matter throughout the report. Unfortunately, this is

Elaine Freeman stands at high east track, cut turf and inadequate work on drain, 25 September 2004.

allied to the quashing the enforcement notice by the Reporter, and must be of serious concern to the public. The related implications for the landscape in such situations cannot be underestimated.

Adam Watson, Alexander D. Walker and Rodney E.F. Heslop, 1 March 2007

Technical suggestions for reinstatement at the Balmore-Auchtavan track

Had the Council's enforcement notice been implemented without delay, it would have been feasible to return excavated material to its site of origin, thus greatly reducing the impacts on scenery, run-off and soil erosion. Now, however, after a delay of two plant-growth seasons, to excavate spoil along the downhill side would cause a severe scar. Nevertheless, we consider it feasible and reasonable to implement the following measures, to reduce the impact of the works:-

An unnecessary excess of bare track occurs along the track's length, and is particularly wide at the bends in the middle section, where it has led to serious run-off and erosion further down, including erosion rills. The width of the driving surface should be cut to a maximum of 3 metres, except for a few passing places and turning bays. This should be achieved by delineating both edges with boulders placed on the track surface approximately every 2 metres. This would serve as a clear visual cue for drivers. Over many years, such a method was used successfully at Cairngorm Ski Area to restrict track width. It greatly reduced run-off and erosion on the track surface, thereby reducing the amount of sediment which was being washed downhill on to vegetation and was killing many plants. Following the narrowing of the Balmore track, the rest of the bare surface on either side would be no longer compacted by vehicles, allowing plants to colonise more readily and stabilise the ground.

An excavator should be used to re-grade the uphill bank by backfilling much of the ditch and reducing the bank's gradient to no more than 30 degrees. Move any boulders dislodged during this operation to borrow-pits as described in paragraph 4. This would stabilise the bank, reduce run-off and erosion, and increase the rate of plant colonisation as in 1. The sole exception should be where any watercourse or flush occurs immediately above the bank. In any such area the re-graded bank should include a French drain, leading to an existing culvert. There should be a sediment trap on the upper end of the culvert pipe, armoured with boulders to reduce water speed. The pipe's exit should be similarly armoured with boulders, to reduce splash and erosion, and where possible should be chosen carefully to coincide with an existing watercourse or flush on the downhill side of the track.

With the exception of watercourses or flushes as outlined in 2, all other culvert pipes should be removed, and the resulting gaps filled with boulders and topped with gravel.

Use an excavator to gather all remaining boulders lying on the surface, move them to existing borrow-pits, and cover them with subsoil. If no topsoil is available, cover the subsoil with a layer of 10 cm of peat.

Given the relatively fertile colluvial soils on the uphill side along most of the track, the shelter from the trees, the comparatively low altitude, and the southerly aspect, there should be no need to re-seed with grass, or to use fertiliser and lime. On the flat section towards Auchtavan, which has much heather and few trees on the uphill slope, the soils are more infertile than in the bichwood, but the gradient of the slope is so low that there is very little risk of serious run-off and erosion. Nature can and should do the healing.

Adam Watson, Rodney E.F. Heslop and Alexander D. Walker, notes by Dr Adam Watson typed on 16 October 2007, final draft agreed by all three on 21 October 2007.

Critique of Reporter's decision letter on Slugain track, 2006

In the following account, the number at the start of each paragraph below refers to that of the numbered paragraphs in the Scottish Executive Inquiry Unit Reporter's decision letter.

3. In this section the Reporter gives her own observations, including, 'The first 60 metres of the track from its junction with the Gleann an t-Slugain track is completely new....The remainder of the track has been formed on the route of a previous path/track.' The first quoted statement is correct, the second inaccurate and misleading. She adduced no evidence for her claim, which is manifestly false. Aerial photographs at SNH's Aberdeen office prove that no previous track or path was there, and a letter by Isla Martin of that office to the Reporter stated this. Also, the Reporter's reference to 'a previous path/track' is incongruously vague in what pertains to be an objective account.

Looking down Gleann an t-Slugain to Slugain Lodge from former footpath that forms the outer edge of new track caused by vehicles and minor engineering, new inner edge wet and muddy, December 2001.

Vegetation and soil torn by Argocat near Well of the Lecht, Crown Estate, author on upper left, June 198

18. Invercauld Estate's appeal claimed that a track had been there for a number of years. As stated above and by objectors, photographs prove the estate's claim to be false. The Reporter ignores this, demonstrating unacceptable bias towards the estate.

20. After admitting that parts of the track have a detrimental impact, she adds that in other parts 'the track is not offensive and fits into the landscape well'. Because she is not an acknowledged expert in landscape, her opinion lacks credibility. Any crudely engineered track offends the many who value wild land.

21. As there is a specific 'policy on vehicle hill tracks (Env\21), I do not consider that local plan policy Gen\2 is particularly relevant'. She then conflicts with her own assertion by giving the policy no relevance.

23. National Park policy 24 has a presumption against hill tracks. Because the Plan has not been to a public inquiry, the Reporter claims, 'it is by no means certain that the final policy will take this form. Therefore, I do not attach much weight to....this policy'. Far from giving it much weight, she then gives it no weight.

24. After noting objectors' rejection of the claim that the track was for agriculture, she adds misleadingly, this is 'beside the point, as use of the estate for sporting purposes is a perfectly legitimate land use'. Objectors stated that the track was illegitimate, not that the sport was illegitimate. The Reporter's assertion here is highly reprehensible because it misrepresents the objectors' statements.

20. The Reporter asserts that track edges 'appear to have' slipped into the burn. It is biased to state 'appear to have slipped', when track edges have undoubtedly slipped into the burn. Her vague suggestion here conflicts with her definite statement in 3. that 'It was evident at the site inspection that in some places the edges of the track have collapsed into the burn', i.e. not 'appear to have slipped'.

She claims there are 'no large areas of cut and fill', but does not define 'large areas'. Photographs by objectors show many steep banks of infertile glacial subsoil, where soil erosion and run-off are inevitable consequences of crude work. Locations in photographs can be verified by comparison with large-scale Ordnance Survey maps, along with inspection of landmarks such as screes, slope steepness, and bends in the burn.

Annex 1. The person to supervise remedial works 'must be an appropriately qualified path worker'. A tracks expert is needed for a track, not a 'path worker'. Her claim reveals profound lack of understanding of the technical issues.

On the site visit the Reporter said she would inspect only the track described in the retrospective application. That recently engineered sections lay beyond was ignored, even though one section penetrated a Site of Special Scientific Interest. The Reporter insisted on restricting herself to the track as a track. She would not consider what objectors called 'the bigger picture', i.e. any track engineered in that side-glen severely obtruded on wild land, and many regard road-less vehicle-free wild land as of priceless value to mankind.

On the site visit she travelled several miles as sole passenger in the front seat of an Invercauld Estate land rover driven by estate factor Simon Blackett, the very body that appealed. This involves a perceived lack of independence and impartiality in the Reporter. Objectors shared the same vehicle, but in the back, and so the Reporter's conversations were predominantly with Mr Blackett, initiated by him.

She is the second Reporter in a year to quash Aberdeenshire Council's rejection of crude unauthorised Invercauld tracks and to ignore the Park Authority's views. The Authority challenged the first decision, a Court quashed the decision, but the same Reporters Unit is now to re-determine it! This last point is unacceptable, lacking any semblance of independence and entailing a conspicuous conflict of interest.

The Scottish Executive created National Parks, but ignorant Executive Reporters undermine the Council's and Park Authority's efforts to care for wild land.

At a meeting of the Marr Area Committee of Aberdeenshire Council in December, it was agreed to challenge this biased decision by the Reporter, and to call on the Environment Minister Ross Finnie MSP to end this shambles by determining the matter himself. It was agreed that a letter be sent to the Scottish Executive's Chief Planner, outlining the Council's grave concerns. The Council agreed to ask West Aberdeenshire MSP Mike Rumbles to help resolve this matter by taking their concerns to the Minister.

'The North East Mountain Trust requests that Mr Rumbles as the local MSP should take NEMT's concerns to the Minister. The NEMT, representing 17,000 citizens of the North-East through member clubs, is at one with Aberdeenshire Council and Cairngorms National Park Authority in wishing high standards for wild land of national value.'

'It is deplorable that two different Reporters from SEIRU within one year quashed the democratic decisions of Aberdeenshire Council when it attempted to maintain standards for planning permission as a necessity for constructing engineered vehicle tracks. Two Reporters have rewarded Invercauld Estate for twice flouting the need for planning approval.' Yet the fact of planning consent being necessary was brought to the attention of Invercauld Estate factor Simon Blackett in the publication *The Angry Corrie*, long before the Estate excavated the Slugain track without planning permission.

'The NEMT calls on Mike Rumbles MSP, the Chief Planner, SEIRU, and Minister Ross Finnie to take decisive action immediately to end the unsatisfactory situation over unauthorised crudely engineered vehicle tracks, and thus better respect the land and the public of Scotland'.

Dr Adam Watson, 18 January 2007

F. Site inspection of Fungle track south of Ballochan

I visited this for two hours on a sunny mild afternoon (13 December 2005) without frost, after several days without rain. Along a distance of 3.3 km, a former vehicle track has been upgraded using an excavator. The vehicle track ended at approximately 508872 near the southern of the two Burns of Allalees, and further south a footpath continued to the county boundary. The footpath went up a steep hillside and had become wider and eroded, as walkers and narrow machines such as Argocats had formed new lines.

The upgraded route follows the original vehicle track throughout, and follows most of the line of the former footpath, but on the steepest section of the latter it takes a new line in a zigzag. Some decades ago, a wide trench was excavated some metres to the west of the vehicle track and roughly parallel to it, starting at about 519889 and continuing down to the Burn of Allanstank. The intention was obviously to divert surface run-off on the hillside from reaching the track. However, it was a highly damaging move, leading to much erosion, and on much of the route was unnecessary, either because in some sections the hillside does not slope upwards west of the trench, or because in some sections the soils are freely drained. The ground has now recovered, with a complete cover of vegetation and no bare soil.

I concentrated attention on the former vehicle track, and I did not have time to walk all the way to the county boundary. I therefore have no detailed notes on the footpath, other than to state that the surface appeared through binoculars from a distance to be of firm gravel, and the zigzag is obviously a better route than the original widening path. In particular I was not close enough to inspect the drainage works on the path section.

The new works on the track involve some addition of gravel extracted from elsewhere, but only on a tiny proportion of the total length. On many sections of the track, the vegetation in the middle of the track has been excavated and deposited at the side. This is perverse, because it has created a far greater extent of bare ground, and worse erosion is inevitable, especially on the steeper parts. The main works involved drains cut on the up-slope side, diverting through culvert pipes to drains down-slope at right angles to the track. A substantial proportion of the up-slope drainage is unnecessary, mainly where the soils are freely drained, but even where the ground is flat and the soils are freely drained, as on the first level grassy section south of the field.

Further south on the moor, where soils are mainly peaty podzols or iron humus podzols, the drainage cuttings on the up-slope side are too deep, cutting through iron pans and through other indurated layers. The result is that the cuttings will bleed run-off from entire slopes uphill from the track. They should not have gone deeper than the first indurated layer. Up-slope drains were left at a near vertical angle, in places overhanging. This is unstable, and already there is major slumping of gravel from the walls into the drain. At about 519889, the drain on the up-slope side is up to 1.2 m deep, presenting a near vertical wall of subsoil.

With frost action and rain, the up-slope drain-walls will slump silt and gravel into the drain, and will then be liable to block the top end of each culvert pipe. No silt traps or traps for other sediment were installed above each culvert pipe, and no pipe entrance was protected to prevent entry of sediment, vegetation and stones. This is a serious flaw. The outlet exit of each pipe was by contrast well supplied with a flat stone to prevent splash and erosion by water.

On the down-slope side of each under-road pipe or other drain, the excavator had dug a wide hollow, generally about 10 square metres in extent of bare ground, but in places up to 30 square metres. This was grossly in excess of what was necessary.

In general, there was excessive removal of turf and dumping of it elsewhere. The handling of heather turf was very poor, and almost all heather turves have died, leaving unsightly grey stems. When old heather was dug out, the thickness of the sod was a mere 5–7 cm, which severs too many roots and results in desiccation of the leaves and then death of the plant. The sod under tall heather should be at least 20 cm thick, and in the abundant peaty podzols in the area and the occasional peaty gleyed podzol, it is easy to cut a thicker sod of 25–30 cm, which ensures good reinstatement.

In most cases the diameter of pipe at 30 cm was in excess of what was necessary, and in one case near the north end the insertion of a smaller 15 cm pipe in a freely drained flat area was again excessive.

In contrast, inadequate attention was paid to drainage on the track surface itself, and this has already led to erosion rills and sediment washed off the road on to vegetation. On one level section in boggy ground towards the north end, the track is a trench with high walls on either side. Clearly it has always been wet, and the surface was muddy during my visit despite several dry days. The obvious remedy here is to remove the down-slope wall in enough places, associated with drains running off towards the burn, so that water does not pond on this sump section. Instead, the lower wall has been added to, using turves excavated from elsewhere, which merely exacerbates the problem. On this section there should also have been a better attempt to raise the surface of the track by adding freely drained gravel from fluvio-glacial sources, which are common. Alternatively, a new route could have been taken to avoid these problems, and the old route then reinstated.

In one place towards the north end, turves excavated recently were dumped at the side. The soils had been cultivated and were very fertile. This material should have been carefully saved for use in reinstating other sections.

On a few sections towards the north end, the soils on the track area are too fertile, with high humus content, and have been churned by vehicles and to a far lesser extent by walkers. This material should have been removed for use in reinstating bare banks, and a more gravelly material used in replacement.

To sum up, although the works have improved the surface of the track, serious problems of track surface and track erosion remain unattended, and some that existed before have been exacerbated by increasing the extent of bare ground on the track. Most of the drainage works were excessive and unnecessary, and have caused greater adverse impacts on soils, vegetation and landscape than what should have been specified. Upslope drains were generally cut too deeply and too steeply, leading to bleeding of run-off over a bigger area uphill than before. The vertical walls of subsoil are already slumping, and none of the upper entrances to culvert pipes has been protected from blockage.

The operation would have benefited greatly from a prior reconnaissance by someone skilled in assessing soils, soil hydrology, and vegetation. If such a person had been transported by a 4 wheel drive vehicle, the inspection need not have occupied more than a half day, and the specification for the works could have been altered accordingly. The work demonstrates ignorance of such technical issues. It was folly to cut through iron pans and other indurated layers, and evidently exploratory pits were not dig with a spade as an essential prerequisite. The excavator driver should have been accompanied by a skilled person on day one. UDAT should alter its procedures, for this is an example of work that could and should have been done much better, especially on an ancient right of way route. A soil reconnaissance would also have resulted in less unnecessary work and hence less cost than the excessive engineering and earthworks carried out.

Dr Adam Watson, 14 December 2005

G. Author's correspondence with Chief Planner James Mackinnon

On 21 December 2005 I sent a letter to the Scottish Executive's Chief Planner Mr James C. Mackinnon in Edinburgh. Below, I reproduce the relevant parts of my letter and of his reply on 5 January 2006.

Dear Mr Mackinnon

I write about vehicle hill tracks. Grampian Regional Council asked me to survey these in the early 1980s for use by planning departments in the area. I published a short account on the survey in a paper in the Journal of Environmental Management. Since then I have kept a register of new tracks in the area and have included some controversial ones in other parts of Scotland.

The issue of these tracks has come to a head in the last few years in Aberdeenshire, where estates have made new tracks or greatly widened existing ones, without planning applications. Generally the work has been done to crude low standards, resulting in maximal impact and minimal reinstatement,

One of the worst cases was the destruction of the historic Old Military Road at Corgarff by Candacraig Estate in 2002. Aberdeenshire Council requested a retrospective application, and would probably have given consent, with conditions attached on reinstatement. The estate refused, and the Council did not pursue enforcement. Although the estate agreed to follow recommendations made after site inspections by Sandy Walker (soil scientist and former senior officer of the Grantown office of the Macaulay Institute for Soil Research) and myself, two years passed before the estate did any work and little attention was paid to the recommendations.

At two other cases in 2002, Gleann an t-Slugain on Invercauld Estate and at Culblean Hill on Dinnet Estate, the Council planning service asked for retrospective applications and eventually recommended full planning permission, provided that the estates took certain actions to reduce impacts and increase reinstatement. At the Marr Area Committee of the Council last Tuesday, Councillor Jenny Watson proposed that permission for the Invercauld track be refused, and this was carried unanimously. She proposed the same for the Dinnet one, but the Committee voted 7 to 2 to give permission with conditions on reinstatement. The new sections in the Dinnet tracks were only a few hundred metres long, and some argued that this was not like a new track, as at Slugain. However, Council planners had ignored new tracks elsewhere on Invercauld and Dinnet that hill walkers had reported and objected to, and ignored extensive engineering for widening and drains on other existing tracks.

In spring 2005, Invercauld Estate carried out extensive engineering works on a track from Balmore almost to Auchtavan in Glen Feardar, inside the Deeside National Scenic Area, involving widening, culverts, ditches and large-scale earthworks, without a planning application. The Council served an enforcement notice, because this was a clear breach of planning regulations. The estate's tenant appealed and the Reporter carried out a public inquiry including a site visit, and then quashed the enforcement order and gave permission, with minor conditions involving some cosmetic reseeding.

Some of the Reporter's statements demonstrate profound ignorance of the technical aspects of the subject. It surely is long past time that individuals with such a power of authority of yea or nay should have at least a basic grasp of technical aspects of soils, hydrology, erosion, vegetation, mitigation and reinstatement. I was astonished when I saw his decision letter and realised the depth of ignorance and bias that were its hallmarks. I therefore made a site visit in November with soil scientists Sandy Walker and Rodney Heslop. The notes from that inspection are attached below.

The Cairngorms National Park planners in Ballater are dismayed by the Reporter's findings, as are the Council planners, and the Park planners are challenging the fact that the Reporter did not pay the attention to the Park that was due. I have sent the two attachments to the Ballater planners, who find them extremely helpful.

I send attachments to you for information, and hope it will be possible to tighten the regulations on tracks. With proper zoning there would be a presumption against tracks in certain areas outstanding for landscape or wildlife, and recommendations that existing tracks in such areas be removed or subject to greatly improved reinstatement. Organisations such as the North East Mountain Trust will not let the present situation continue without frequent comment, and adverse public criticism of Councils and Executive is inevitable until the public interest is served.

People see a stark contrast between firm action against householders who erect a garage or dormer window without planning consent, and even against housing developers who are forced to demolish flats built slightly off the agreed alignment, and the cavalier disregard of crude tracks made by estates for miles up beautiful glens. Objectors who were heard at the Marr Area meeting said this, that there seemed to be two rules, one for the average citizen, but carte blanche for estates. There can be no defence of the unfair inconsistency in such a situation. It seems likely that housing developers may take legal action against enforcement, and point to estates being let off the hook. This is not good for democracy or public regard for good planning.

Although objectors have criticised Aberdeenshire Council for inconsistency and lack of action, the fact is that it is one of the very few Councils in Scotland, perhaps the only one, with a clear explicit policy on such tracks. Highland Council territory is open house to such tracks, unless they are in National Scenic Areas.

I know that tracks for agriculture and forestry are permitted development, but this has for years been a glaring anomaly. These are not the sacred cows that they necessarily were during the second world war and shortly afterwards, and the days of maximising subsidised farm production and timber production, irrespective of the costs to taxpayers and third world agriculture, are disappearing rapidly, and will soon be gone.

It is possible to make new tracks with minimal impact and maximal reinstatement, and there are excellent examples, such as the new road made across Priestlaw Muir in the Lammermuir Hills in connection with a new power line from Torness reactor. The technical information on how to do this is well known, and some contractors do an excellent job. Most contractors can do a good job if that is insisted upon, and the cost need not be materially much greater than doing a quick dirty job.

5 January 2006
Dear Dr Watson

Thank you for your letter of 21 December. You will appreciate that it would not be appropriate for me to comment on individual cases but I thought I could usefully pick up on some of the general issues that arise from your letter.

The first point relates to the skills and knowledge base of the planning profession. The nature of planning is such that officials, and indeed elected members, are expected to develop quite detailed understanding of a whole range of issues and their impact on the environment. Some of these are very technical and highly complex, including the formation of hill tracks in certain circumstances. To address what we perceive are potentially significant skills and knowledge gaps we have allocated £2.25 million over the next few years to support the upskilling of the planning profession. We are in the process of appointing a manager to take forward this programme.

The second point relates to planning controls over vehicle tracks. As you say, these are currently permitted development. You should, however, know that we are carrying out a major review of permitted development as part of our drive to modernise and reform the planning system. In essence we are asking fundamental questions of what should and should not require planning permission. There are many developments, often very minor, which appear to be perfectly well regulated through consent regimes other than planning so why require people to obtain 2 authorisations when one will do. We also recognise, though, that there will be pressure to extend controls, and vehicle tracks for agriculture and forestry is one such area. The consultants carrying out the review are led by Professor Alan Prior at Heriot-Watt University. You may wish to write to Professor Prior with your views on this as I am sure it is an issue that will feature in the consultants' report.
Yours sincerely
James G. Mackinnon,
Chief Planner

Postscript by Adam Watson.
I did write as he suggested. The Scottish Executive had commissioned Heriot-Watt to review the Scottish planning system, and the review became public in 2006. The consultants recommended radical changes in planning legislation over the long-outdated anomaly of Permitted Development Rights for agriculture and forestry, including vehicle tracks. Five years on, the Scottish Government has not acted on the recommendations (McNeish 2011).

H. Critique of SNH 2006 report *Constructed tracks in the Scottish uplands*

First impressions of this 'good practice guide' (ISBN 1 85397 468 4, Scottish Natural Heritage, Battleby, Redgorton, Perth) are good, because of the attractive layout, aided by colour-coded sections and a glossary. Unfortunately the guide is unnecessarily wide and awkward for a bookcase or use in the field, and the pages take up less than half the space in the large ring-binder.

Section 7 on Planning and Legislation

This summarises the regulations. Although Section 7 will be a useful source for many readers, it suffers from over-emphasis on stating known facts, and unwillingness to criticise obvious failings or anomalies. A good example is on p. 127 on Planning Consents, where one finds accurate factual statements about exemptions through the General Permitted Development Order. For example, the middle column includes the following, "Class 18 allows for the formation, alteration or maintenance of private ways on agricultural land where this is required for the purposes of agriculture". A second example is in the right column, "Proposals within forests managed by Forest Enterprise Scotland are not subject to the same level of scrutiny and there is no consultation on individual elements such as tracks. Furthermore, as part of the Crown Estate, Forest Enterprise Scotland is legally exempt from planning controls though it is required to submit a Notice of Proposed Development to the local planning authority before work commences." There follows no comment on these two anomalies or their potential consequences in causing serious damage to landscape, wildlife and amenity, and no such comment elsewhere in the guide.

The authors do not point out that the General Permitted Development Order is a euphemistic term for allowing many potentially damaging developments without planning control by local authorities or central government. Despite a conspicuous lack of explicit clarity in the regulations more generally, the guide fails to emphasise this or its consequences. The most obvious consequence is that different planning officers inevitably vary in their interpretation of the perhaps deliberately woolly phrasing of some regulations.

Over-emphasis on landscape and wildlife

One of the main flaws of the guide is that the detailed reasoning and recommendations about making tracks are usually lost within a text emphasising landscape, landforms and wildlife. There is also heavy use of unnecessary jargon such as 'biodiversity', 'geodiversity', 'the natural heritage', 'ecological resource such as blanket bogs' (p. 51), and 'design out' (p. 38). An absurd example on p. 38 is the term 'ecological receptors'. One reads 'Valuing (should be Evaluating) those habitats and species likely to be affected by a development (known 'in the trade' as 'ecological receptors') allows avoidance measures to be prioritised on the most valuable biodiversity features'. The term 'in the trade' could hardly be less useful in persuading practical people on the ground that those who wrote and oversaw the text share any identity or common-sense thinking with them.

After this comes a table on p. 39 where the term ecological receptors is in the title, with no quotation marks and no cross-reference to the attempted explanation on the opposite page, and no inclusion in the Glossary at the end of the book. The Table places overwhelming emphasis on statutory designations, and splits the 'Level of value' into Highest and Lowest, with no intermediate category.

Other general problems with the text

The result of the overemphasis on landscape and wildlife, and also the jargon-ridden text, is that the practical person who wishes to make a track will find the book frustrating and largely irrelevant. This is exacerbated by the inclusion of footpaths with vehicle tracks. The front cover adds to this confusion by having the major photograph showing two walkers on a narrow footpath, and the minor photograph showing a shepherd walking with sheep on a track instead of showing a vehicle.

The text of the manual suffers from frequent unnecessary repetition, which renders the text unnecessarily long and tedious.

At the start, the guide notes that there has been an increase in the demand for new tracks on hill land in recent years, but ignores the well-known fact that most of the bulldozed or excavated vehicle tracks were made in the late 1960s and early 1970s. The concerns raised by conservationists about this rapid proliferation of generally poorly constructed tracks led to a report by the Countryside Commission for Scotland in 1978, a reference ignored in the current SNH report. The CCS report in turn led to regulations in 1980 to control new tracks in National Scenic Areas (reference under Scottish Office in the current report). The current report also ignores the survey of vehicular hill tracks in Grampian Region and nearby land in 1981–82, initiated by Grampian Regional Council, and leading to a paper on the survey, published in the *Journal of Environmental Management* (Watson 1984). In short, the introductory part of the new report is inadequate and belies ignorance of the subject on the part of the authors and the SNH staff who commissioned and oversaw the production of this guide.

There is frequently an unstated assumption in several parts of the guide that a route for vehicles requires engineering. Usually no engineering operation with excavators is required on freely drained soils, if the vehicle use is to be restricted to land rover and other light vehicles, but this is usually ignored. Following this guide will inevitably lead to greater impacts and expenses than are necessary.

The use of cargo helicopters for lifting turbine components and other material required for wind-farms and other construction projects is not even considered. If this were feasible, it would reduce environmental impacts enormously.

The list of consultees at the end includes not a single soil science department or section in a university, or in an agricultural department or college, or in any other relevant state-funded organisation. It includes only one contractor, which seems unnecessarily restrictive and unfair to other contractors.

Imported soil for surfacing

One of the salient factors that make vehicle tracks and paths more conspicuous than they need be is the use of imported material for surfacing. Such sources outwith the site often contain subsoil that has been derived from a different kind of bedrock or a different type of glacial deposit than that on the site. The manual does touch on this point, but does not give it the emphasis that is needed. A good example is the photograph of a footpath, on the front cover of the guide, in which imported material on the path has created a conspicuous ribbon that is completely out of place in that landscape. The land shown in the photograph clearly lacks such a colour of subsoil, as can be inferred from the bedrock in the photograph. It seems likely that this photograph was taken in the Inchnadamph area, or in a part of the Highlands with similar climate and bedrock, where the subsoil is darker and would not have produced such a prominent scar.

A further issue about imported material is that the guide does not warn against using fluvio-glacial or riverside alluvial sand for surfacing. Both are loose and highly permeable, lack binding qualities, and are too easily displaced by feet, bicycle wheels, vehicles, and rain. Such loose material is readily shifted on to vegetation, thus extending the damage and leading to eventual dieback. It is also inconvenient for walkers, because the loose material readily gets inside footwear. An example is the resurfacing of the path along the second hillock west of Luibeg by the National Trust of Scotland in August 2002, using fluvio-glacial sand and gravel.

Many works on paths and tracks in recent years have involved surfacing with loamy sand, which looks not only out of place on routes in woodland and moorland, but readily erodes. After rain followed by frost, the surface becomes icy, posing risks to walkers and cyclists. A current example is the path work carried out in August 2006 at Anagach Wood near Grantown-on-Spey, a wood owned and managed by a local community trust.

The work at Anagach involved tracked vehicles, another unnecessary cause of extra damage, and was counterproductive and damaging to landscape and wildlife, because the original paths were in good condition and self-cleaning; only minor works were required by hand at wet spots. Unfortunately the end result was unnecessarily large expanses of sand where several paths met, thus killing much vegetation and leaving too much bare ground. Erosion rills 5 cm deep and associated sediment fans had already occurred by 8 September. Some of the eroded sand had washed on to the surface of the Wade Military Road.

Detailed comments

p. 5. The impacts of tracks on wildlife are treated entirely one-sidedly. In fact, tracks are favoured by many vertebrates and invertebrates because they offer dry warm sites, shelter, and cover, e.g. for chicks of waders and grouse after rain. The report ignores this well-known point.

p. 9. The statement 'Tracks should only be constructed where absolutely required' is irrelevant, because those who make tracks would not do so unless they thought it was required.

p.13 and 79. The need for a site survey is mentioned, but does not specify that this must entail work by experts experienced in soils, hydrology, vegetation and reinstatement, and that it should be preceded by a careful stereoscopic inspection of aerial photographs of the proposed route. The guide should have stated where libraries of such photographs are kept, such as the national archive at the Royal Commission on the Ancient & Historical Monuments of Scotland, as well as in regional archives such as Grampian Regional Council's archive, now held by Aberdeenshire Council, and regional offices of SNH.

Furthermore, a survey of the route should entail a prior inspection of the soil maps produced by the Soil Survey of Scotland, part of the former Macaulay Institute for Soil Research, and available from the new Macaulay Land Use Research Institute at Aberdeen. It is a surprising oversight that these maps, which were produced in coordination with the Ordnance Survey and have long been available for sale, are ignored.

This lack of emphasis on the necessity of careful, rigorous survey is a crucial flaw. Those who read this section could readily conclude that anyone, such as a gamekeeper or estate factor, could do the survey. On p. 79, stress is put on a 'Thorough site survey is required at an early stage to determine ground conditions...Investigations may include the use of trial pits to determined the depth of surface deposits.' Instead of being 'at an early stage', an obligatory site survey should be done before anything else. Also, soil profiles dug by spade would have been a more useful phrase than trial pits, as the latter could be interpreted as pits dug by an excavator. This section completely ignores the fact that the main point of the site survey is not to determine 'surface deposits' (again, a jargon term that will not be readily understood by non-scientists), but to determine the optimum line for the track, in terms of minimising impact and maximising reinstatement. This includes searching for sections of freely drained ground where no excavated track may be needed if use is to be by 4 x 4 vehicles and not a lorry.

p. 47. 4th sentence. Native pinewoods also occur on steep slopes, such as in Ballochbuie, Glen Strathfarrar, and Inshriach.

p. 52. Foot of page. It is stated that 'montane soils, peat and calcareous or magnesian soils are among the most valued in Scotland'. This uses the term 'montane' to mean what is generally recognised internationally as 'alpine', there being almost no montane vegetation in Scotland in the internationally accepted sense. This paragraph ignores the iron podzol, which is much rarer than alpine soils or peat, yet is the foundation for much native boreal woodland and moorland.

p. 63. The one page on climate is inadequate, giving little on thunderstorm rainfall and thaws, and strangely singling out south-west Scotland as a region that is considered likely to receive more rainstorms due to climatic change.

p. 72, 76 and 90. Drawings. A cut-off ditch on the uphill side of a track is stated to be 'as required'. This is another serious flaw, because it ignores the fact that such a ditch in freely drained soils is unnecessary, and may be counter-productive because it can lead to extra run-off and erosion. This is even worse where the cut-off ditch penetrates below an iron pan or an indurated horizon. In such cases the ditch would subsequently concentrate water situated on a perched water-table. Water running immediately above the pan or individual horizon could thus be bled from uphill slopes Also, the gradient shown for the uphill and downhill re-graded banks is the maximum that should be allowed, to achieve stable conditions. This is not stated.

No mention is made of the drainage problems associated with ditches dug on sites with a high ground-water table as opposed to the perched water-tables described above.

p. 80. Rock types. 1st paragraph. The glossary has no explanation of 'metamorphic'. Also, it would be useful to give a reference to the Geological Survey's Ten Mile Map, North Sheet.

3rd paragraph. Sands and gravels are not rock types.

In the section on rock, there is no mention of weathered rock, yet this is good material for making tracks.

Photographs. There are too many on fine landscape and wildlife, and too few giving examples of poorly made and well made tracks, and of different relevant features of soils and vegetation types. In total there are 98 photographs, only 53 of which show tracks, so almost half (46%) of the photographs involve subjects other than tracks. Surely the proportion covering tracks should have been overwhelmingly preponderant, such as 80% or 90%, not 54%. The photograph on p. 4 has a captions 'Tracks can be prominent features in the upland landscape, detracting from wild land qualities'. This is ironic, because the track shown is in Strath Dionard, and the Countryside Commission for Scotland objected, but NCC was in favour and SNH later allowed the track. Under a heading on 'Landscape and visual effects', a photograph on p. 20 shows the Lairig Ghru from Rothiemurchus. This is inappropriate, because there is no track in that area or shown in the photograph, and the prominent scar in the photograph shows a landslip that followed flash-flooding during a thunderstorm.

p. 87 The drawing shows cambered ditches on both the uphill and downhill sides of the track. This ignores the fact that such ditches on either side are normally unnecessary on freely drained soils. Also such ditches on the downhill side of the track are vulnerable to collapse. Furthermore, the re-graded bank on the uphill side as shown is far too steep for stability.

p. 88. It is stated that a smooth base to a ditch 'will minimise the risk of erosion'. The opposite is the case. To reduce erosion, the speed of the water flow must be reduced, which is impossible with a smooth base. A base roughened with stones, as in a stream, is required to reduce water speed and consequent erosion. Then it is stated that gradients of ditches 'should be steep enough to allow efficient drainage, but not so steep as to create erosion'. Such vagueness is regrettable in a technical document intended to aid those who construct tracks.

p. 89. The drawing of a culvert exit shows one boulder well above the surrounding level, to reduce the speed of water leaving the culvert. This is inadequate. The culvert exit should have several boulders forming a rough platform.

One reads that culverts should be made where streams or 'natural drainage channels cross the track route, and at regular intervals between these points'. This is inadequate. It fails to define 'natural drainage channels' in a way that would be readily observed to anyone in the field. The text here should have mentioned flushes or groundwater seepage, readily conspicuous by the vegetation. Secondly, it should have been mentioned that, depending on the width of the flush, more than one culvert may be needed. Thirdly, there is no need for culverts at regular intervals between streams or flushes if the soils are freely drained, and indeed in such soils there is no need for any culverts at all. Nothing is stated about the level at which the culvert entry should be placed, in relation to the groundwater or stream. Nothing is said about the importance of choosing safe routes on the downhill side for water to debouch from culverts and down-slope roadside ditches, or how one can choose such routes on the basis of the topography and the vegetation.

Table 7 in the SNH report lists the advantages and disadvantages of different types of drainage, but leaves the reader unaware of the preferred option.

p. 99. On the timing of the works, the report deals entirely with avoiding disturbance to animals, and gives nothing on the best timing for reducing impacts to ground and vegetation, and for maximising reinstatement. The latter impacts on habitat are far more important for wildlife populations than temporary disturbance of a small number of individual animals. Worse, this section leaves unstated that the best season for constructing tracks is in spring, to take advantage of a full growing season for natural reinstatement. This should be April for low moorland, and preferably early May at the latest for high moorland, provided that the ground is not still waterlogged. The authors mention that those who construct tracks should avoid wet (undefined) or very dry weather, but weather is largely irrelevant. The important issue here is ground conditions. There is nothing wrong with making a track on a wet day if the ground is not waterlogged, provided that one obviously avoids a day of heavy rain.

p. 100. It is stated that 'reseeding may be necessary', again an unacceptable vague phrase. If vegetation removed during construction is properly kept, there is bound to be enough of it to cloak all exposed banks, indeed often an excess of it. There is therefore no need for reseeding. Many clients and contractors pay lip service to this, and destroy most of the vegetation and topsoil or peat during the course of excavation and reinstatement. In *The Scotsman* of 9 September 2006 (p. 15), a photograph of a wind-farm and associated road on Scottish moorland illustrates the problem well, for the roadside banks and ground immediately around the turbine bases have hardly any vegetation and comprise bare peat mixed with some subsoil. This clearly indicates that most vegetation was destroyed, because there should have been an excess.

Nothing is stated here about different soil types, apart from the vague statement that 'subsoil' should be kept separate from topsoil or peat, and vegetation. There is nothing on the value of retaining the upper section of the B horizon for use in reinstatement (because of its fertility), or of the need to separate the B from the C, or about the importance of storing these horizons separately and putting them back in reverse order. This section mentions 'dry weather' as being useful, but earlier on p. 99 stressed the need to avoid 'very dry weather'. This is potentially confusing, and again clouds the important issue of soil wetness with current wet weather.

p. 101. One reads that excavated stored soils should be kept 'damp'. The use of this word indicates the report authors' lack of expertise on soils. Then it is stated that soils should be stored for 'a maximum of 1–2 months'. This is absurd, and contradicts the earlier statement that work on putting back soil and vegetation should be done, section by section of excavation, rather than being left to the end. In any case, no track is going to require 1–2 months for construction. Most are done in a few days. It is a crucial flaw to ignore the need to insist upon reinstatement work to proceed in very close tandem with excavation, indeed within the day for each section.

p. 103 on Soils is particularly inadequate, and fails to mention salient issues noted in the comments above.

Apparently the Cairngorms National Park Authority has sent copies to estate owners in the Park. A good opportunity has been missed, through inadequate knowledge and also insufficient care in commissioning and overseeing of the project by SNH. A revised edition could redress most of the flaws, by utilising properly the technical expertise available on this important subject.

Adam Watson, Sandy Walker and Rodney Heslop, 2 February 2007

Note

In the latest issue of *The Scottish Mountaineer*, the newsletter of the Mountaineering Council of Scotland, a review of the SNH publication has been contributed by Mike Newbury (2006). After summarising the adverse effects of uncontrolled tracks on the landscape, he writes 'Does this SNH publication help? Sadly, it does not. There is a sensitive and beautifully illustrated portrayal of wild landscapes and habitats, making this at first glance a splendid publication, but it is virtually all within the context of "Strategic track design" and "detailed track design and construction" occupying 101 pages, i.e. "How best to build more tracks", against 4 pages on "Questioning" (less than rigorously) "the need for tracks and exploring alternatives" and 6 pages on "Track enhancement and restoration", including a single page on removal....the constructional guidance offered here is less than thorough, judging by publications already available and the best current practice'.

Information from MC of S added by AW, ADW & REFH, 2 February 2007

On 27 May 2010 the *Deeside Piper* newspaper carried a report about a meeting of landowners in the Cairngorms region, held at Aboyne. Aware of rising publicity about the need for planning controls on vehicle tracks and of a debate on this in the Scottish Parliament in early June, the landowners did not wish planning controls and argued that guidance on best practice would be enough. The above SNH document was cited as providing that guidance, and SNH and the Cairngorms National Park Authority stated that they would help. It should be realised that the SNH document certainly does not provide satisfactory guidance on best practice, and the above reviews by Watson, Walker and Heslop make this indubitably clear.

I. Cairngorms Group 1974, *Bulldozed private roads in the Cairngorms*

The report with this title is reprinted below. It was written by Norman Keir, Sandy Payne and Adam Watson in 1974 and was issued by the Cairngorms Group, forerunner of the North East Mountain Trust. It led to action by the Countryside Commission for Scotland, too little too late. Reading it in 2011 indicates the little progress that has occurred since 1974.

Nature and extent of the problem

The Cairngorms Group, a 50-strong Group within the Aberdeen Branch of the Conservation Society, wish to send you this open letter which states their objections to the continuing proliferation of private bulldozed roads in the Cairngorms and other outstanding hill areas of Scotland. About 1000 miles of these roads have been built by private landowners in the last decade, to make easier access for shooters of grouse and deer.

A few of the bulldozed estate roads have been well made to a high standard like that of Forestry Commission roads, and so have caused little scarring of the landscape; they last well, and their banks soon recover with vegetation that stops erosion effectively. However, most private bulldozed roads have been built carelessly, without proper drains and with the spoil left in large untidy heaps; these roads have led to considerable soil erosion and are obvious scars on the landscape, in some cases showing as ugly ribbons even at ten miles distance. This would be serious enough at low altitudes and on ground of low amenity value, but many roads have been built high into the fragile arctic-alpine zone where vegetation is very easily damaged and takes many years to recover, and where erosion is severe. Others have been built into quite outstanding areas of high-quality scenery where the roads are ugly scars that spoil the fine views. Some of these roads have also led to massive litter appearing in remote places where rubbish is difficult to clear, such as a complete tractor dumped and now broken-down at 3600 feet on the high top of Beinn a' Bhuird. It seems inappropriate to us that, although planning permission is required for a new building, there is no public control of these new bulldozed roads, most of which are far more serious intrusions on a hill or moorland landscape than any building. Other roads have been bulldozed into National Nature Reserves of international significance and into Sites of Special Scientific Interest, a development which we deplore and which we feel to be wholly undesirable for these valuable, specially-protected areas that occupy such a tiny fraction of the country. In addition, some of the last small major remnants of trackless "wilderness" which are left in Britain and are significant in a European context have been progressively and relentlessly infringed by these new roads.

Finally, many attractive walking paths, including some on outstanding old rights of way such as Glen Feshie and Glen Derry, have been ruined permanently by the bulldozing of new roads along the exact lines of the old paths. As these fine old paths are a magnificent heritage of the Scottish people, we fully agree with Tom Weir's description of the bulldozing of them as "this kind of vandalism" (*The Scots Magazine* 101, p. 252). Unfortunately, these acts are not all a matter of the past, as every year sees new private roads being made; for example, in late 1971 much of the remainder of the beautiful path in Glen Feshie was bulldozed by an extension, so that the entire length of the old path through the Old Caledonian pine woods there has now been totally destroyed. It is surely paradoxical that age-old public paths are disappearing under the bulldozer at a time when the Secretary of State for Scotland has recently authorised the building of a West Highland Way footpath, said to be the first long-distance footpath to be built in Scotland. The recognition that such a path is necessary as a recreational facility is itself a condemnation of the present trend in destruction of footpaths to convert them into roads for land-rover use.

Proposals for action

We fully accept that much of the hill ground in the Highlands is not of high scientific, scenic or amenity value and is seldom visited by people, for instance on many of the lower hills and grouse moors. Accordingly, we think that it would be unreasonable if not impracticable to ask for the same blanket controls on these roads over a very large area like the Highlands. What we do suggest is the following scheme, whose aims would be mainly to protect the most outstanding places but also to encourage the development of better road standards elsewhere. It is based on a zonation of the Cairngorm area in terms of National Nature Reserves, Areas of Great Landscape Value, etc., and a weighting according to the relative values of the different zones. These zones fall inside a critical area, convenient boundaries for which are suggested as follows.-

Feshiebridge - Nethybridge - Tomintoul - Corgarff - Strathdon - Dinnet - Glen Tanar - Tarfside - Milton of Clova - Spittal of Glenshee - lower Glen Tilt - Glen Feshie.

All the most outstanding hill country in north-east Scotland or east of the A9 road would be included in such an Area. It is intended that the guidelines presented below would also have applicability over other sensitive areas in Scotland where such developments are taking place.

1. As a control on private bulldozed roads, the Group asks for an Article 4 Direction of the General Development Order (Town and Country Planning Act 1972) to be submitted to the Secretary of State for Scotland by the present County Councils or the appropriate planning authorities that are soon to replace them. We suggest that the Countryside Commission for Scotland initiates the moves that would lead to this action. The Group feels that this ad hoc measure is not wholly satisfactory as there is obviously a need for a much wider, detailed and comprehensive policy that will account for other present and future demands and problems, among which the current problem of bulldozed roads is only one aspect among many. Nevertheless, the Group recommends the short-term ad hoc measure, for all its defects, as it would be a method of tackling the problem of the bulldozed roads immediately and as it is now imperative that some action be taken.

2. Looking at the many other conservation problems of the area in a wider context, the Group strongly supports the incorporation of the Cairngorms massif (already partly covered by National Park Direction Area status) within a designated Area of Special Planning Control following Section 9 of the Countryside (Scotland) Act 1967. The landscape policies for the Area of Special Planning Control would of course include the construction and siting of new private roads.

The Group fully realises the particular difficulty of administration for an Area of Special Planning Control in the Cairngorms. The area of the Cairngorms massif and the hill country and glens around it lies astride the boundaries of the Grampian, Highland and Tayside Regions, and many boundaries at District Council level. Additionally, District Councils within a given Region may well adopt different tactics or standards of development control in achieving the policies formulated by the Regional Council. There is therefore a case for either an independent agency (possibly headed by staff from the Countryside Commission for Scotland), or for some joint local authority board (perhaps headed or serviced by CCS staff). Study Group 9, which was the instrument for setting up the Countryside Commission for Scotland, envisaged one of the Commission's roles as being responsible for areas designated as National Parks. The Study Group expected the CCS to have the staff, the knowledge and the finance to administer these areas in the way that National Parks in England are managed. In addition to these, other bodies would need to be consulted, such as the Department of Agriculture and Fisheries for Scotland, the Nature Conservancy Council, Forestry Commission, and Highlands and Islands Development Board. Because there are so many different organisations, the consultation that will be necessary before an appropriate comprehensive structure can be set up is likely to take much time. This is another good reason why a short-term measure - such as suggested in 1. above - is required for the immediate problem of the bulldozed roads. An Article 4 Direction of the General Development Order (Town and Country Planning Act 1972) would be only an interim, short-term measure but it could be implemented now, until the many problems of creating an Area of Special Planning Control in the Cairngorms have been resolved carefully and with more time.

3. For any road to be built within a National Nature Reserve or Site of Special Scientific Interest, prior agreement would be required from the Nature Conservancy Council and the District Council.

4. For any road to be built within an Area of Great Landscape Value or any future designated Area of Outstanding Natural Beauty, prior agreement would be required from the Countryside Commission for Scotland and the District Council.

5. For any road to be built within a local Nature Reserve, a Scottish Wildlife Trust Reserve, a Reserve of the Royal Society for the Protection of Birds, or important archaeological site, permission would be required from the District Council.

Author on Hill of Modloch checks new tracks by Millden Estate, Glen Esk, June 2010.

Catherine Lacy and Brian Heaton of North East Mountain Trust use camera and GPS to survey Druim Cholzie track, Glenmuick Estate, looking towards Hunt Hill, 31 May 2009.

6. For any road to be built along a right of way or public path, prior agreement would be required from the Countryside Commission for Scotland and the District Council.

7. In other areas, which would in fact cover by far the bulk of the Highland hill around in terms of total acreage, the building of new private roads should be made a subject for consultation procedures between the landowner, the Countryside Commission for Scotland and the District Council. The aim would be to try to increase the standards of building and maintenance of these roads towards the standards which have already long been used and maintained by the Forestry Commission on its own forest roads. This would probably have the effect of reducing the excessive proliferation of roads and cutting them down to what is really necessary, as well as inculcating a better sense of stewardship of the countryside than has existed over the last decade.

8. Any applications for agricultural subsidy from public funds to help pay for new bulldozed roads on deer forests and grouse moors should be more carefully investigated. In a few cases on deer forest, this Group feels the applications were not justified as the roads have been used almost entirely for sporting purposes and very little - if at all - for agriculture.

9. A detailed survey of existing private bulldozed roads should be made, so as to re-evaluate them. Dr A. Watson at the Institute of Terrestrial Ecology, Blackhall, Banchory, has already completed a survey to show on a map all the bulldozed roads in the area, but what is needed now is a detailed survey of the state of these roads, including such aspects as mileage of footpaths destroyed, mileage in National Nature Reserves and other special areas, erosion, drainage, and vegetation damage. This would be followed by either reclamation or proper maintenance, reclamation back to the original vegetation being a serious suggestion for a few tracks that have been bulldozed in National Nature Reserves and Sites of Special Scientific Interest. Dr N.G. Bayfield at the Institute of Terrestrial Ecology, Brathens Hill, Banchory, is already doing a small selective survey of this kind, and the Countryside Commission for Scotland might be the appropriate body to build on this research and to help expand it.

We call on the Countryside Commission for Scotland, as the most appropriate agency, to initiate discussion and arrangements that will put proper public control on the individual's current licence to bulldoze these roads anywhere without planning permission. The most outstanding parts of the Highlands occupy a very small proportion of the total area, and in many respects are magnificent heritage. This heritage is now being irreparably damaged over a very short period of years, and urgent action is required now, in the long-term interests of the Scottish people, if the heritage is to be worth anything to future generations.

Cairngorms Group
c/o 8 Esslemont Avenue, Aberdeen
8 November 1974

Postscript May 2011, roads for access to the Beauly–Denny power-line

After a Public Inquiry, the Scottish Government decided that a high-voltage power-line will be constructed from Beauly to Denny near Stirling. The route crosses moors, woods and bogs in areas valued for scenery, wildlife and tourism. New roads will be needed for lorries so that pylons and cables can be erected. Readers can see in the internet under Beauly–Denny power-line the full details including an Environmental Impact Assessment. A *Construction Procedures Handbook* (CPH) is obligatory, and the current draft of it is in the website of Scottish and Southern Energy.

On soils and ground vegetation the CPH is vague and inadequate, referring for example to 'best practice' several times, yet not defining it or stating details. Its references to the storing of soils and turfs according to 'best practice' show that reinstatement will come long after excavation. For instance it states that turfs should be put into ditches to prevent the plants drying out, an impractical and counter-productive comment. It stresses a good grass seed mixture, and that reseeding should not result in prominent green stripes in the landscape.

The CPH states that advice will be taken from Scottish Natural Heritage and the Forestry Commission about road construction and ground reinstatement, but that advice should already be in the CPH. In any case, the government's statutory adviser SNH cannot be relied upon for sound advice on hill roads or tracks, because the SNH report (2006) *Constructed tracks in the Scottish uplands,* a 'good practice guide', is so inadequate and signified a surprising lack of the relevant technical expertise within SNH. Even worse, FC roads involve near-total destruction of vegetation and upper soil horizons along the affected route, as well as highly obtrusive scars in the landscape.

Given the wide roads and affected ground on either side, there is bound to be a big surplus of vegetation and upper soil horizons. Hence there is no excuse for work that destroys most vegetation and upper horizons, or leaves excavated boulders and lower soil horizons on the surface. Storage of soils and extant vegetation should proceed daily in tandem with excavation, so as to maximise reinstatement, and without any need for obtrusive grass reseeding. Reseeding is an unsatisfactory palliative after failure to respect and use the big surplus of natural soils and vegetation available along the route.

The present book under the auspices of NEMT clearly states the measures that need to be taken to minimise impacts and maximise reinstatement, in detail. It rests on fundamental lessons from soil science, vegetation ecology, and hydrology. These have been well tested and should be heeded. Many will be watching.

Latest news 22 June 2011

A former track up to the top of Cairn Leuchan on Glenmuick Estate has been freshly surfaced, conspicuous from the Bridge of Gairn even 7 km away. The Scottish Rural and Property Business Association, renamed eight years ago from the Scottish Landowners' Federation, is now again renamed Scottish Land and Estates.

CPSIA information can be obtained
at www.ICGtesting.com
Printed in the USA
2389LVUK00003B